The Stepping Stones Journals

The STEPPING STONES JOURNALS

Written by
DIANA R. JENKINS

Pauline
BOOKS & MEDIA
Boston

Library of Congress Cataloging-in-Publication Data

Jenkins, Diana R.
The stepping stones journals / by Diana R. Jenkins.
  p. cm.
ISBN 0-8198-7129-X (pbk.)
1. Diaries--Authorship--Juvenile literature. 2. Diaries--Juve-
nile literature. I. Title.
PN4390.J46 2010
808'.06692--dc22

2009032317

Cover art by Chris Sabatino
Art on pages 57, 61, 71, 75, 89 by Chris Sabatino
Book design by Mary Joseph Peterson, FSP

Published by Pauline Books & Media, 50 Saint Pauls Avenue,
Boston, MA 02130-3491

Printed in the U.S.A.

SSJ VSAUSAPEOILL03-1009-09457 7129-X

www.pauline.org

Pauline Books & Media is the publishing house of the
Daughters of St. Paul, an international congregation of women
religious serving the Church with the communications media.

1 2 3 4 5 6 7 8 9   13 12 11 10

Contents

Mrs. Lewis
First Period English
St. Paul Catholic School

The Journal Project

Keeping a journal is a great way to improve writing skills! For the first grading period, we'll all be writing regularly in personal journals. (Yes, me, too!) Here are some guidelines for this special project:

1) You may write about anything—your life, your family and friends, your feelings, your dreams. It's up to you!

2) We'll set aside some class time for journal writing a couple of times a week. You *must* write in your journal during this time.

3) You *can* write in your journal at other times during school or even at home, if you wish. You'll find that the more you write, the more your writing will improve.

4) Journals are private! You can share what you've written with others or keep it to yourself. I will read your journal only with your permission. Please respect the privacy of other students' journals.

5) Do your best on spelling, punctuation, and grammar, but don't get hung up on those things. You'll be graded on your participation and effort, so relax and let your thoughts flow!

Week One

Wednesday, August 20   *Suki's Journal*

    I think these journals are a great idea! I really want to be a better writer. It will help in school, of course, but writing is important for my future, too. I'm planning to make movies when I grow up. I've been getting a lot of practice with my camera. Like I make videos for the school TV station. And I've already made a couple of movies called *First Day of School: The Movie!* and *Youth Group: The Movie!* I guess you could say they're documentaries. I filmed real people doing real things, and I learned a lot about filmmaking when I did them. But wouldn't it be cool to write scripts and direct actors in my own movies??? I'll have to be a great writer to do that!!! I'm going to write in this journal a lot so I can really improve my writing skills.

Wednesday, August 20   *Chantal's Journal*

    I'm going to write about my BIG NEWS! Next Wednesday I'm starting my first real PAID babysitting job. I've watched my little sister, Amanda, before, but that wasn't a job. Wait . . . it WAS a job because it was work, but it wasn't a REAL job because Mom and Dad didn't pay me. I didn't mind because she's my sister and we almost lost her because of her heart trouble and

I'm just glad to have her. But I'm excited that I'm going to have a real job now. I'll be watching a first grader on Wednesdays and Thursdays after school until his parents get home. And they're going to PAY me! I'm a little bit nervous, but I know I'm ready. After all, I work with lots of kids when I volunteer at the church nursery and the hospital playroom. And I'm going to be a teacher when I grow up. I know how to handle kids. Harrison is so sweet—I'm sure he won't be any trouble.

Wednesday, August 20 *Alberto's Journal*

This is going to be a good year. I like my schedule and all of my teachers. I get to be around my friends all day long. And the best thing is I already made the football team! We have been practicing twice a day for three weeks. It's been really tough practicing in the hot weather. Now that school has started, we'll have to cut down on our practices, but that's okay. Our team is really in good shape now and Coach Pulaski thinks we'll have a good season. We have our first game after school tomorrow, and I can't wait! I hope I get to play!

I'm starting to be good friends with the other guys on the team. Even Osmond has been friendly to me. He used to pick on me a lot and tease me when I had my weight problem. Back then I would never have dreamed we could be friends. But now I think we can. It's great being part of a team!

Wednesday, August 20 — *Denver's Journal*

I don't know what to write I don't know what to write. I don't know what to write. I don't know what to write I don't know what to write. I don't know what to write. I don't know what to write I don't know what to write. I don't know what to write. I don't know what to write I don't know what to write. I don't know what to write.

Friday, August 22 — *Chantal's Journal*

My parents drive me CRAZY! I understand that there have to be RULES and they are the PARENTS and they are RESPONSIBLE for me but do they have to treat me like I'm a little child it is RIDICULOUS!

When I got home yesterday, I just wanted to relax. We've only been in school a few days and I'm not used to it, okay? Things are going fine, but I was kind of tired and a little stressed. I NEEDED to relax. So I broke one of Mom and Dad's big rules. I didn't start my homework right away. Instead, I watched TV awhile. Well, you would think I committed a CRIME! Dad got on my case and then Mom came in and griped me out and then they both lectured me for an hour. Hey, I could have done a lot of homework in that time.

I have always tried to make good grades and be a responsible student so it wasn't like I was NEVER going to do my homework. I was planning to do it later. What's wrong with that? Why can't they trust me to decide stuff like that for myself? After all, I'm old enough to start a real job. Maybe when they see how I handle my babysitting job, they'll realize that I'm more mature than they think. I HOPE!

Friday, August 22   *Alberto's Journal*

WE WON OUR FIRST GAME YESTERDAY! I wasn't too excited about that at first because the coach didn't put me in. I sat on the bench the whole game. (I'm going to have to practice really hard!) But Osmond and some of the other guys asked me to go out for pizza after the game. It was like it didn't matter that I didn't play because we're all a team.

We had so much fun at the restaurant. Ray told a joke and Yazid laughed so hard he snorted soda out of his nose. Then everybody started blowing straw wrappers at each other. And the funniest thing was when Joey wasn't looking and Osmond loosened the lid on the cheese shaker and then Joey tried to shake cheese onto his pizza and ALL of the cheese fell out. It was so hilarious we cracked up for ten minutes!

I'm starting to have so many friends. And that feels great!

Friday, August 22   *Suki's Journal*

Yesterday I decided to join the staff of the school newspaper. I'm very serious about becoming a good writer, and working for the paper should really help me. Hey, maybe I'll have two careers!!! I could work on my movies and become a reporter, too. Maybe even on TV!!! Maybe I'll travel to other countries and film important events and write up reports and then appear on camera and give my reports!!!

As soon as I joined the newspaper, Mrs. Pyle gave me the job of covering the first football game that afternoon. Our team won, but Alberto didn't get to play for even one second so I couldn't write anything about him. Which was a good thing in a way because he was too busy for an interview after the game. He was hanging around with the rest of the team and I waved at him, but he didn't even notice me. It didn't really bother me because it's nice to see he has lots of friends on the team and he is having fun. Alberto used to get picked on a lot when he was over-weight. I'm glad people have started to see how nice he is. And, of course, I'm glad he's healthy enough to play sports now!!!

I am writing in my journal. I am writing in my journal. I am writing in my journal. I am writing in my journal. I am writing in my journal. I am writing in my journal. I am writing in my journal. I am writing in my journal. I am writi

Week Two

This morning we had the first meeting of the French Club and something très bon happened!!! (That means "very good" in French.) Mademoiselle O'Reilly said we needed to elect a president and people started nominating other people for the job and Madison raised her hand and nominated me. Then we voted and almost everyone voted for moi!!! (That means "me" in French.) I couldn't believe it!!! I thanked everybody then suggested we get right to work on fund-raising. When we have some money together, we can think of something fun for the club to do. Hopefully something that involves French food. I love trying food from different countries!!!

It's just so cool how my life is going!!! I'm doing all kinds of great stuff. I volunteer at the nursing home and I make videos and I write for the newspaper and now I'm the president of a club. C'est magnifique!!! (It's great!!!) After I joined the newspaper, my grandparents warned me not to do too much. They said they don't want me to get "overwhelmed" and "tired out." Sometimes they worry about me too much because I'm in a wheelchair. But I can do just about anything!!! And what's one more activity? As long as I can keep up with everything—which I can— why shouldn't I live life to the fullest???

DATE: AUGUST 26, 7:14 PM
FROM: CHANTAL
TO: SUKI
WHERE R U? Y NOT @ YUTH GRUP?

DATE: AUGUST 26, 7:29 PM
FROM: CHANTAL
TO: SUKI
U R MISSN YUTH GRUP!

DATE: AUGUST 26, 8:05 PM
FROM: CHANTAL
TO: SUKI
ALMOST OVR!

DATE: AUGUST 26, 8:31 PM
FROM: CHANTAL
TO: SUKI
U MISSD IT!

DATE: AUGUST 26, 8:45 PM
FROM: SUKI
TO: CHANTAL
SORRY DEDLINE 2MORO HAD 2 FINSH ARTICL

Thursday, August 28   *Alberto's Journal*

I'm so stupid! When the coach called an extra practice yesterday, I completely forgot I was supposed to meet Denver at the park. And after practice I went right past the park, but I was running through some plays in my mind and

I still didn't think of Denver. I didn't even remember about him until this morning when he asked, "Where were you yesterday?" Then it hit me. I told him I was sorry and he said it was okay, but he's mad. I can tell. It was just a mistake! Sometimes I wish he'd loosen up a little and be more fun. Like Osmond and my other teammates. They are always doing something funny!

Like at lunch yesterday, Osmond asked Ray, "Hey, what's that in your mashed potatoes?"

"What?" asked Ray.

"That!" Osmond pointed.

"What?" said Ray.

"That! There!" Osmond pointed again.

Then Ray bent over to get a closer look and Osmond pushed his head down into the mashed potatoes. When he sat back up, he had mashed potatoes all over his face! We all cracked up. Even Ray. He can take a joke. If you did something like that to Denver, he'd probably clobber you! Well, maybe not. He's a lot better at controlling his temper than he used to be. But I bet he'd be really mad about it.

Thursday, August 28   *Denver's Journal*

abcdefghijklmnopqrstuvwxyz abcdefghijklmnopqrstuvwxyz abcdefghijklmnopqrstuvwxyz
abcdefghijklmnopqrstuvwxyz abcdefghijklmnopqrstuvwxyz zyxwvutsrqpomnlkjfedcba

It's a good thing I'm getting paid for babysitting because the first day was not fun AT ALL! I was supposed to pick Harrison up at his bus stop, walk him home, give him a snack, help him with any homework, have him read to me, then play if we had time. That kid would NOT cooperate. As soon as he stepped off the bus, he started begging to go to the playground and he wouldn't stop even though I told him again and again that his parents wanted us to go home. I decided to just not answer him any more, but then he said, "Can't you hear me?" And when I didn't answer, he started yelling at the top of his lungs, "CAN WE GO TO THE PLAYGROUND? I WANT TO GO TO THE PLAYGROUND! LET'S GO TO THE PLAYGROUND!" So I had to start talking to him again.

When we got to his house, things didn't get better. He didn't like the snack I made even though his mom had told me cheese and crackers were his favorite food. He read his book at super speed and got half the words wrong. When I made him go back and read more slowly he went like, "Oooooooooooo-kaaaaaaaaaaay. Iiiiiiiiii'll reeeeeeeeeee-ad slooooooowerrrrrrrrr." Aaaaaaaaaaaaa! It drove me CRAZY! By the time I finally got him to do it right, his father was coming in so there wasn't time to play anything. We didn't have any fun AT ALL!

I didn't tell his dad about his behavior because I figured I give him another chance. But I'm worried about how he's going to act today. I told Suki everything and she said, "Remember how you had trouble with the kids in the nursery to start out? That didn't last. I'm sure you'll work it out." It was such a nice thing to say that I decided I'm not mad at her anymore for missing youth group. I DO think she's doing too much stuff. Missing youth group proves that. I told her how I feel, but she just shrugged me off.

Thursday, August 28  *Suki's Journal*

I don't know why, but Chantal is making a big deal out of me missing youth group. It was just one time, but she says I'm getting too busy. That is ridiculous!!! I have several activities going on, but it's not a problem at all!!! There's nothing wrong with being active!!!

Friday, August 29 ★ ★School News★ ★

Come to Le Café de Paris!!!
Enjoy delicious treats at the French Club Bake Sale!!!
Wednesday, September 10

Friday, August 29 *Chantal's Journal*

AAAAAAAAA! Harrison acted up again yesterday! That kid argues about EVERYTHING! Maybe babysitting isn't going to be as great as I thought it would be. It WAS nice when Harrison's mom paid me! It felt good to be making my own money.

Tonight we're all going to the football game to watch Alberto play. I hope the coach puts him in the game.

Friday, August 29 *Suki's Journal*

I went online and found a lot of good recipes for fancy cookies and cakes and stuff. They looked très délicieux!!! (That means "very delicious"!!! I'm getting really good at speaking French!!!) I'm planning to make several of them for the French Club bake sale. Hey, maybe I'll be a chef one day. I'll be a TV reporter and write my own scripts and make movies AND run my own restaurant where I'll prepare gourmet meals. I'll be famous for my French pastries!!!

Friday, August 29 *Denver's Journal*

Denver Denver Denver Denver Denver Denver
Denver Denver Denver Denver Denver Denver
Denver Denver Denver Denver Denver
Denver rules the world! Denver Denver
Denver Denver Denver Denver

I've really been working hard at practice.
I hope hope hope the coach puts me in tonight!
The guys didn't seem to care that I sat the
bench before, but I'll feel more like part of the
team if I get to play.

It happened! I finally got to play! It was
only for a little while, but it felt great to be
helping out my team. And we won again! The
coach says he is really proud of how hard we're
working.

After the game, Suki, Chantal, and Denver
came up and went, "Alberto! Alberto! He's our
man! If he can't do it, no one can!" Then they
jumped up and down going "YAY!" It was pretty
funny—and nice, too. My little brother, Esteban, clapped for me and my parents were
really proud and they took us to a restaurant
to celebrate. It was great!

DATE: AUGUST 30, 2:15 PM
FROM: ALBERTO
TO: CHANTAL, SUKI
DENVRS BDAY NEXT WK. GO 2GETHR ON GIFT?

DATE: AUGUST 30, 2:18 PM
FROM: CHANTAL
TO: ALBERTO, SUKI
GRB IDEA!

DATE: AUGUST 30, 2:21 PM
FROM: SUKI
TO: ALBERTO, CHANTAL
IM N!

DATE: AUGUST 30, 2:25 PM
FROM: ALBERTO
TO: CHANTAL, SUKI
ILL GET SUMTHNG GUD FROM FUN SHOP

Week Three

Hi Suki!
From Justin and Lee

My brothers are such pests!!! A journal is private it's not something for them to be fooling around with!!! It's personal!!! But they don't understand the meaning of the word. They won't let me have my own personal life. No, they have to bother me all the time!!! Like they always want me to play a game. Or read them a story. Or listen to them talk, talk, talk!!! I have plenty of better stuff to do.

I told my grandparents that the boys keep bugging me, but they weren't any help. Grandma just said, "But they're your little brothers, Suki. Of course, they want to do things with you! You should be happy about that."

Then Grandpa frowned at me and said, "Are you too busy to spend time with your family?"

And I said, "No, but Justin and Lee are big pests!!!"

Grandma and Grandpa said that wasn't true.

But now I have proof they really are pests because only pests would get into somebody's journal. But I guess I can't show my grandparents the proof because then they would see this stuff I wrote. Rats!!!

Over the weekend, I went to the Fun Shop to get a birthday present for Denver. Suki and Chantal gave me some money so I could get something good from all of us. I thought maybe I could find a funny present that would make Denver relax a little and have some fun. Like my football friends!

It wasn't easy to pick something. First, I thought I'd get him some candy that looked good but tasted like fish. How hilarious would it be when he tasted that? But then I thought it would be funnier to get some fake puke and wrap it up in a big box. He would have to laugh at something disgusting like that. But then I saw the Big Birthday Box of Fun and I decided that was the perfect gift for Denver. It looks like a normal birthday present all wrapped up with a bow on top, but when Denver takes off the lid, a fake snake will pop out. I can't wait for him to open it! It's going to be so funny even Denver will have to laugh!

I AM NOT A BABY!!!

I told my parents that yesterday and they said of course not, but I know they don't mean it. They DO think I'm a baby and they treat me like one. Like I don't get to stay up that much later than Amanda! And my parents are so ridiculous about my bedtime. Like last night all I wanted to do was stay up a LITTLE late to watch a movie. They told me to record the movie and go on to bed because it was a school night. Like I didn't know that! I said couldn't I stay up and it wouldn't be that late and I could handle it and stuff like that, but they kept saying no. Then Dad said that children need their sleep which is true but the way he said it made me sound like I was THREE YEARS OLD! That's when I yelled that I wasn't a baby and they said of course I wasn't but they sent me to bed anyway. They can SAY I'm not a baby, but as long as they do stuff like that I'll know they don't really believe it.

The next time they treat me like that, I'm going to bring up my babysitting job. If I'm mature enough to babysit a little kid for actual money then I'm mature enough to make my own decisions. So far I haven't said much about babysitting just that it's going fine but really the second day wasn't any better than the first day. Harrison didn't want to do anything I told him. And I had to tell him to do stuff again and again before he'd do what I said. But I'm determined to make that kid behave! And after I do, THEN I'll tell my parents how well I'm handling my responsibilities and they'll have to give me more freedom.

Tuesday, September 2   *Denver's Journal*

boring boring boring boring boring boring boring
boring boring boring boring boring boring boring
boring boring boring boring boring boring boring
boring boring boring boring boring boring boring
boring boring BORING!!!!!!!!!!!!!!!!!!!!!!

Wednesday, September 3   *Alberto's Journal*

Yesterday we had another game and Coach Pulaski put me in again, but for longer this time I made some good tackles and he said I did a great job. He's really a nice coach. We won again, and this time I felt like I helped a lot more. All my hard work is paying off!

After the game, we went to the locker room. Osmond made a big water balloon and chased us all around, threatening us. I escaped him once by jumping up on a bench, running along it, and hopping off at the end. But later he caught me near the water fountain and bombed me. It was so fun—and funny! I'm going to have to think of a good trick to play on somebody because pranks are like our team thing. And I'm part of the team!

Wednesday, September 3   *Suki's Journal*

I almost got in trouble yesterday—at school!!! I got to math class and realized I didn't do our assignment. I couldn't believe it!!! I guess I just got so busy with other stuff that I forgot.

Mr. Evans noticed that I didn't come up and turn anything in and he called me to his desk and I was afraid I might get detention or something but he said it's the first time ever so just turn it in tomorrow. I was so relieved!!! Now that I'm doing so much I'm going to have to keep better track of everything!!!

Wednesday, September 3   *Denver's Journal*

nothing to write nothing nothing nothing
nothing nothing nothing nothing nothing
NOTHINGNOTHING NOTHING!

Wednesday, September 3   *Chantal's Journal*

My parents are so out of it! It's like they live in the PIONEER DAYS! All I did was put on a little lip gloss before I left the house this morning. And just a little eye makeup and some blush. You could hardly even SEE it. But they got all upset and asked where did I get all that like they thought I STOLE it or something! Then I told them they were some free samples that Madison gave me and I explained that her mom sells makeup so they have lots of free samples like that. Then Dad said, "Well, you're TOO YOUNG for makeup!" And Mom said, "Go wash it off!" I knew they wouldn't listen if I said anything back and anyway the bus was coming soon so I just ran to the bathroom and did what they said. It's RIDICULOUS how they treat me.

DATE: SEPTEMBER 5, 7:30 PM
FROM: CHANTAL
TO: SUKI
DENVRS BDAY PAR T STARTNG! WHERE R U?

DATE: SEPTEMBER 5, 7:46 PM
FROM: CHANTAL
TO: SUKI
RU COMING 2 PAR T OR NOT??

Saturday, September 6   *Denver's Journal*

Wow! That was the best birthday party
ever! And the biggest, too! I couldn't believe
it. As friend after friend after friend came
in the door last night. Everybody I knew
was there. Well, Suki was late, but at least
she made it! Lately she's so busy we
hardly ever see her.

Anyway, we had all this fantastic food
that Mom made for us—all my favorites!
We had pizza and nachos and chili dogs and
homemade onion dip and all kinds of stuff!
We ate and talked and played music and
then Mom brought out a huge chocolate cake
with candles. Of course, everybody sang to
me and I blew out the candles and then we
had cake and ice cream.

After that, everybody wanted me to open
my gifts. I got a lot of nice presents
and even one funny present from Alberto,

Chantal, and Suki. (Too bad Suki didn't see me open it. She still wasn't there yet!) When I opened their gift, a snake popped out and scared me to death!

My mom always gets me good presents, but this time she gave me the best gift ever! It's this handheld game I really, really, really wanted. It's called Zplutz! The idea of it is to work your way through all these mazes until you finally get to a treasure. It wasn't that hard at first. I'm already to the second level. But then the game started getting tougher! Like in the mazes on the first level, it didn't matter if I turned the wrong way. I could just turn around and go back. But now if I turn the wrong way, a trap door opens up and I fall through back to the lowest level and the game makes this funny sound like ZPLUT!! It's a tough game, but it's great! I don't think I'll ever get tired of it.

Saturday, September 6   *Chantal's Journal*

I cannot believe Suki! She came so late to Denver's party last night that I don't know why she bothered to come AT ALL! She wasn't there when he blew out his candles. She missed the cake and ice cream. She didn't see him open any of the presents. It was funny when he opened OUR present, but Suki missed that. By the time she finally rolled in, there wasn't even much food left. Not that she noticed! She came up to a group of us and started making a big deal about all the things she has to do. SHE volunteers at the nursing home and SHE makes videos for the school's TV station and SHE'S the president of the French Club and SHE writes for the newspaper and BLAH BLAH BLAH! It was unbelievable!

I finally couldn't take it anymore. "Okay, okay," I said. "You're so important. We get it already."

Then she got mad and said, "I didn't say that! I'm just busy, okay?"

I was going to say some more stuff, but some other people were looking at us and I realized I shouldn't make a scene at Denver's party. So I just said, "Okay. Whatever." I don't think I could have changed her attitude anyway. She just doesn't get it that she's TOO busy—and that's not something to BRAG about. She pretty much missed a FRIEND'S birthday party. That's not right!

Week Four

📖 New Book Club!!!

Do you enjoy reading??? Do you like discussing what you've read??? Come and share your love of books in a new book club!!! For more information, contact Suki.

Tuesday, September 9   *Denver's Journal*

I made it to the fourth level of Zplutz! That was not easy to do, let me tell you. Once I figured out how to get through the mazes with the trap doors, things got even trickier. There were still trap doors if you went the wrong way, but also there were secret stones you had to push to make a door open to the next maze. And if you pressed the wrong one, you got dropped back to the first level again. Finally, I figured out you had to choose the stones that had exactly three symbols on them. Once I started doing that, I was able to move through all the mazes on that level pretty quickly. I can't wait to see what happens on the next level!

Alberto came over yesterday and I explained the game and let him play it while I got us something to drink. When I came back, he said, "Oh, no! I think I broke it!"

I almost dropped our sodas! But then I saw he was smiling, and I realized it was just a stupid prank. He is hanging out with Osmond and those other doofs too much. I didn't even smile. I just said, "Funny." Then I took the game back and played it myself and just let him watch until he had to go home. Why should I let him play if he's going to act like that? And what if he fooled around and accidentally broke the game for real? That would be terrible!

Tuesday, September 9   *Alberto's Journal*

I played a really funny prank after football practice yesterday! I was the first guy back to the locker room so I got my bottle of shampoo and waited to the side of the door. Yazid came in and he didn't notice me until I started squirting the shampoo all over his head! He started yelling, "What is that? What is that? Get it off of me!" Everybody else walked in behind him and they all started laughing.

Osmond yelled, "It's just shampoo!"

Ray said, "Yeah. What's the big deal?"

Then Yazid said, "Oh. Okay. I was going to wash my hair anyway."

Everybody kept teasing him for being scared of shampoo. And they kept looking at me and saying, "Good one!"

Yazid stayed in the shower a long time so I

figured I had the chance to pull another prank
on him. I picked up one of his shoes, smelled it,
and said, "P! U!" Then I poured some shampoo into
the shoe. Everybody cracked up! Dad was waiting
for me in the car so I had to leave before Yazid
came back, but Osmond called me later to tell
me what happened. He said I should have seen
Yazid's face when he stuck his foot in that shoe.
He said it was the funniest thing he ever saw
in his life. After that, we talked for a pretty
long time about football and school and other
stuff. We're really getting to be good friends!

Tuesday, September 9   *Chantal's Journal*

I think Suki's mad at me about what happened at Denver's party. She's hardly talked to me
at all. When I see her, she just says hi and rushes
past. All I did was tell her the TRUTH! Friends
can be honest with each other, right? Maybe I hurt
her feelings a little bit, but I'm sure she'll get over
it. I'll try to smooth things over at youth group
tonight.

Tuesday, September 9   *Suki's Journal*

I think Chantal's still kind of mad that I was
late to Denver's party. (Like I could help that!!! I
had to finish making the bookmarks I was taking
to the nursing home the next day!!!) She made
a big deal out of it then and it seems like it's still

bothering her. We haven't seen each other at school much, but she could call!!! Is she too busy to talk to her best friend???

DATE: SEPTEMBER 9, 7:36 PM
FROM: CHANTAL
TO: SUKI
Y R U MISSN YUTH GRUP AGAIN?

DATE: SEPTEMBER 9, 7:39 PM
FROM: SUKI
TO: CHANTAL
SORRY BAKNG 4 SALE. ILL B THERE NEXT TYM!

Wednesday, September 10   *Chantal's Journal*

You know, I used to think Harrison was so cute, but now I just think he's a BRAT! Okay, that's a little strong he's not a brat all the time. But he can really be a PAIN! I've watched him four times now, and things have not gone smoothly even once. He is always arguing with me or refusing to do something or doing the opposite of what I tell him. I can make him do what I want, but I have to say stuff so many times that it stresses me out. And I hate the way he smarts off to me.

Like this afternoon he had a math worksheet to do for homework. It was the easiest math paper EVER, but I had to struggle for an hour to get him to do it. When it was finally finished, he said, "I'm glad you're not my teacher!"

I go, "Why not?"

Then he goes, "Because you're mean!"

Then I go, "I am not!"

Then he goes, "You are too!"

And I go, "No I'm not!"

And he goes, "Yes you are!"

I'm too mature to argue with a little kid so I said, "Let's read your book now." But I'm still really annoyed about the whole thing. I hate it that he would say something about my teaching when I'm planning to become a teacher. And I think I will be a GOOD teacher! IF I don't have students like him.

I have to admit that Harrison can be really sweet sometimes. Like even when he's in a terrible mood, he gets all happy when his parents come home. And he always hugs me good-bye and says, "Seeya!" I just wish I could get control of him! Whenever his parents ask me how things are going I say things are fine—that's what I tell my parents, too. What else CAN I say? If I admit I'm having problems, then it's going to look like I can't handle the job. Harrison's parents might decide to get another sitter. And my parents will be disappointed in me. They've said a couple of times that they're proud of me for being responsible enough to babysit. I CAN'T let them down now!

I'm trying to be hopeful that things will get better, but I feel kind of disappointed myself. This job isn't anything like I thought it would be. And

I'm not looking forward to babysitting this after-noon. It's cool to be making my own money, but I'm not sure it's worth it!

I really wish I could talk to Suki about all this, but—surprise, surprise—she missed youth group AGAIN last night. This morning, she was busy setting up the French Club bake sale so I couldn't talk to her then. She'll probably be work-ing at the table every spare moment today, so I bet she'll never have time for me. She never does any more!

Wednesday, September 10   *Denver's Journal*

Wow! It was really tough getting to the fifth level of Zplutz! Level 4 had all the challenges of the first three levels PLUS the maze would go dark every so often. If I just stood there and waited for the lights to come back on, I'd drop back to the first level. But if I moved on and bumped into something, I got dropped down, too. And if I made any mistakes while I was moving around in the dark . . . ZPLUT! It took for-ever to get through all the mazes on that level and move up I mean it took hours and hours and hours!!

Mom thinks I'm playing the game too much, but if I don't practice a lot then how am I going to get good at it? And it's not like I have much to do anyway. Alberto is

always going to practice or playing a game
or doing something with the guys on the
team. And Suki is so busy I almost never
lay eyes on her. And Chantal is . . . I don't
know . . . stressed out, I guess. It's not
even fun to talk to her any more. It's a
good thing I have my game. I wonder what
problems I'm going to run into on this level?

Thursday, September 11   *Denver's Journal*

New walls suddenly come down and block
the way!

Thursday, September 11   *Denver's Journal*

And old walls suddenly disappear!

Thursday, September 11   *Suki's Journal*

Yesterday's bake sale was a huge success!!!
We'll have to have another one soon. Who
knows??? Maybe we can raise enough money for
a trip to Paris. HA!!! Or at least a trip to a French
restaurant here at home!!!

This morning I tried to talk to Chantal, but
she acted all mad and started saying that stuff
about how I'm too busy and we never do
anything any more. Then she walked off before
I could say anything back.

I was kind of mad at first but then I realized she was sort of right I mean we really haven't gotten together in a while. So at lunch I sat with Chantal and Madison and I said we should meet at the mall on Saturday.

Chantal said real sarcastically, "Are you sure you can make time for that???"

I could have made a remark back, but I stayed calm and said, "Yes, I'm sure. And I really *want* to do it." Then she seemed to feel better and we all started talking about the stores we wanted to go to and what we should eat and all that.

We decided to meet at the food court at 11. I'm volunteering at the nursing home that morning, but I figure Grandpa can pick me up there and drop me off at the mall. When I get back home, I'll work on my stuff for the newspaper, catch up on my homework, and plan my next video. Really, I have a lot to do and I shouldn't waste time at the mall, but I care about my friends even though I'm busy. I hope Chantal appreciates that!!!

Thursday, September 11   *Chantal's Journal*

I couldn't believe it when Harrison actually behaved yesterday! I had to get on him a few times, but mostly he did what I said. He even read his book without goofing around and he didn't smart off at all. Things were finally working out. YES!

But when Harrison's mom got home, she took one look at him and said, "Oh, my! Are you sick,

Harrison?" Then she took his temperature and he WAS! I told her I was sorry I didn't know, but she said it was okay. I still felt TERRIBLE about it! You'd think that after having a little sister with tons of health problems, I would have noticed that Harrison didn't feel well. I guess I was just so happy he was behaving that I didn't stop to wonder why. I'm going to watch him very, very carefully from now on. I don't have to babysit today because his mom kept him home from school. It's kind of a relief, to tell you the truth.

I have some GOOD NEWS! Suki, Madison, and I are meeting at the mall on Saturday. With all the stress I've been having, I could use a fun time with friends. I can't wait to spend my babysitting money. And I'd really like to catch Suki up on what's been going on in my life. It seems like we haven't REALLY talked in a long time.

Thursday, September 11   *Alberto's Journal*

We're Number 1! We're Number 1! We're Number 1! We're the only undefeated team in the area! The coach plays me some in every game now so I really feel like I'm part of the team's success. And even if we don't keep winning, it's okay. I think I'll still feel like a winner because I've made such good friends playing football.

Like Osmond. I used to think he was mean— and sometimes he was! But now we have a lot of fun. He's actually pretty funny. Like yesterday at lunch, he opened a mayonnaise packet and left it on a chair at our table. Then Joey came along and sat down without noticing. Osmond and I were cracking up! Joey asked what was going on, but we couldn't stop laughing long enough to tell him anything.

Then the other guys came along and sat down and asked what we were laughing about. Finally, Osmond got hold of himself and told Joey to stand up and turn around. He did it, and the little plastic packet was stuck to his pants and there was mayonnaise oozing out! Everybody laughed—even people at other tables. Joey laughed, too, then went to the bathroom to clean up. When he came back Osmond pointed and said, "Did you have an accident?" That's when we saw Joey had a big wet spot on the back of his pants, and we all cracked up again. It was so fun!

Thursday, September 11   *Denver's Journal*

That stupid Osmond really burns me up! He's just plain old mean to people—even his own teammates—people who are supposedly his friends! At lunch yesterday he put a mayonnaise packet on a chair and just waited for some victim to come along and sit down. Then Joey who's on the football team with Osmond walked up, but Osmond just let him sit there and get mayonnaise on the back of his pants. Everybody was laughing at the poor guy, and Osmond was teasing him, too.

I felt sorry for Joey. Oh, he tried to act like it was all a joke, but he couldn't get out of there fast enough. I guess he tried to get the mayonnaise off in the bathroom because when he came back his pants were wet. Of course, Osmond had to say stuff about him wetting his pants! I know Joey was way embarrassed.

The really bad thing about it all was that Alberto was sitting right there and laughing along with everybody else. Why does he want to hang out with a jerk like Osmond? I just don't understand it. It's like he doesn't get that Osmond's pranks aren't funny at all. They embarrass people! And hurt their feelings! I'm not surprised about Osmond acting like that, but Alberto is a nice guy. At least, he was before he made the football team.

Saturday, September 13   *Chantal's Journal*

I AM SO MAD AT SUKI! She was supposed to meet Madison and me at the mall at 11. We waited and waited and waited and WAITED! Madison and I were both mad and we talked about how Suki is too busy. I know Suki doesn't agree, but if you are so busy you keep your friends waiting for 45 MINUTES then you are TOO BUSY! I mean that is so DISRESPECTFUL to act like people have nothing better to do than wait around for you!

When Suki finally showed up, did she APOLOGIZE for keeping us waiting? NO! She just started talking about how she got busy on her newspaper article and so she got to the nursing home late so she felt like she had to stay later and oh by the way she couldn't shop too long because she had SO MUCH to do this afternoon. It was like she was the big SOMEBODY and we were little NOBODIES and we should be glad she worked us into her BUSY BUSY BUSY life. I was FURIOUS and I know Madison was, too, but she just said, "It's okay."

Since Madison was acting nice, I took a breath and said, "Yeah, it's okay. Hey, let's go to the bookstore."

The whole time we were shopping, Suki talked about all the stuff she has to do like she was doing us a big favor just being there. She never once asked me how things were going in MY life! After just two hours, she had to go. For the rest of the afternoon, Madison and I shopped and com-plained about Suki and her hot-stuff attitude. I know it's not nice to talk about people, but I think Suki deserved it with the way she's acting. You don't treat friends the way she treated Madison and me!

Week Five

September 15, 3:45 pm

Alberto: What R U doin?

Denver: Online research 4 sci report

Alberto: Want 2 do something l8er?

Denver: Rnt U doing sumthng w Osmond?

Alberto: No want 2 meet at park shoot hoops?

Denver: 2 busy! Need 2 work

Alberto: OK Another tym

Denver: Sure.

Tuesday, September 16   *Denver's Journal*

Alberto actually had a moment for me yesterday. Like one minute he wasn't doing stuff with Osmond and the team! They must have all been busy tricking little children out of their candy or teasing puppies or something or I wouldn't have heard from him. He wanted me to meet him at the park, but I made an excuse for not going. Hey, if he never has time for me, then why should I make time for him?

And anyway I'm busy with Zplutz. I just made it to the sixth level. It's really A-MAZE-ING! Now the mazes are mazes within mazes! Like once you think you've made it through a maze and you're standing at the door to the next maze, you see that there's a maze pattern on the door. You have to pick up a magic pencil and trace the maze correctly in only a few seconds. If you don't well down you go! It's going to take me awhile to get to level 7.

Tuesday, September 16   *Suki's Journal*

Alberto is so rude!!! I got this great idea that I'd interview him about how he got healthy and videotape it for the school TV station. I knew he would have a lot of good advice about nutrition and exercise and all that. When I told him about it he seemed really excited to do it, and we agreed to meet in the cafeteria after school. But when I got there, he was nowhere in sight!!! I was a little late, but he could have waited a bit. But no!!! He just took off, and now I don't have anything for tomorrow's broadcast. I tried to call him when I got home, but he didn't answer his phone. So now I have to do something quick!!! I decided to set up the camera and film myself talking about the new book club. I figure I'll show the book we're planning to read and encourage people to join. Of course, I'll have to miss youth group again to get it done!!! Gee, thanks, Alberto!!! I bet Chantal is going to be mad at me, but what else can I do? At least I spent a lot of time with her on Saturday. She really shouldn't have anything to complain about.

Wednesday, September 17   *Alberto's Journal*

I was supposed to meet Suki after school yesterday, but she never came. She's way busy these days so maybe she just forgot. It really bugged me because I waited around for a long time, but I guess I can be understanding and just let it go. Everybody makes mistakes sometimes. Like what about that time I forgot to meet Denver?

Wednesday, September 17   *Chantal's Journal*

I can't believe that Suki missed youth group AGAIN last night! And when I saw her this morning she didn't explain or apologize or ANYTHING. All she said was "Wait until you see today's video!" Then she hurried off to the office to turn it in and she didn't come back until homeroom was starting so we never even got to talk. It seems like we NEVER do any more! I think Suki is changing. Today her morning video was about HER and HER book club! She used to do videos about other people. I guess because she used to actually CARE about other people.

Wednesday, September 17 *Denver's Journal*

Brother! Suki's video today was all about her! The whole thing! She actually taped herself talking on and on about her book club like she was some kind of big shot on TV!

Wednesday, September 17 *Suki's Journal*

The video came out great!!! I could tell everybody really liked it. I bet a lot of people will want to join the book club now.

I'm glad I have something to feel good about because things were not good at home this morning!!! I was working on some homework in my room and the boys came and said it was time for breakfast. I told them I was going to skip breakfast this morning because I had work to do. That was a big mistake!!! Grandma and Grandpa came and started lecturing me again about how I'm doing too much. Grandma even talked about good nutrition like I don't know that stuff. Finally I said okay okay and went to the kitchen to eat. It's hard to keep up with everything and it doesn't help when my grandparents take up my time like that!!!

Thursday, September 18 *Chantal's Journal*

Sometimes I feel like my life is just one big MESS! Everything is going wrong this week!

Like on Monday, I got a D on my social studies quiz, and my parents FREAKED OUT! They said if I couldn't keep my grades up, then I would have to stop babysitting. I would feel like a COMPLETE FAILURE if I had to do that. I tried to tell them that I just forgot to study the cities of the ancient world and I would improve my grade later, but they thought I was getting an attitude and Dad cut me off and said they didn't want to hear my excuses. Which was SO UNFAIR!

And Suki skipped youth group again on Tuesday, and she hardly even talked to me yesterday. I guess I don't fit into her BUSY schedule! I wish I didn't care, but it makes me feel AWFUL!

So does babysitting. Yesterday on my way there, I prayed and prayed and asked God to make Harrison behave, but it didn't work. He was all well again, and he acted up a lot—to make up for being good last time, I guess. He whined and whined that he didn't want peanut butter toast for his snack. He wanted cheese and crackers! Then he slumped way down in his chair and read his book so quietly that I couldn't hear him. I told him to read louder, but he wouldn't, of course. So I leaned in closer and found out he was going, "Blah blah blah blah." So I made him read the whole story over again!

The worst thing was when he was doing this worksheet about the months. His writing was so sloppy you couldn't even read it. I made him erase everything and do it over. When he started whining about his fingers hurting, I decided I had had ENOUGH of his behavior. I jumped right on him and made him be quiet and get back to work and every time he just opened his mouth I said, "I don't want to hear it!" Because I DIDN'T! But it wasn't a very nice thing to say, and I started thinking what if Harrison complained about me to his parents? So I said, "Harrison, I don't like yelling at you, but you've been a bad boy and I had to do it. I really should tell your parents about your behavior." And he said, "No! No! No!" And I said, "Well, okay, I'll give you another chance." So I don't think he'll say anything to his parents about me, but I feel bad for tricking him like that.

Yeah, my life is a MESS!

Thursday, September 18   *Denver's Journal*

I still haven't made it to the seventh level even after hours and hours and hours trying to get there! And I mean HOURS! I've even stayed up late and played the game with the sound muted so Mom won't notice. The mazes on the doors keep getting trickier and trickier. Like sometimes you have to trace back to the start of the maze before the door will open. Or you might have to tap the magic pencil three times. When you get to the end of the maze. You just have to try different stuff until you find out what works. I've been dropped down a million times! But I'm getting close to defeating this level—I can feel it! I just have to keep working at it.

Thursday, September 18   *Suki's Journal*

Alberto hasn't said anything about missing our interview!!! I can't believe it!!! Isn't he even a little bit sorry??? We haven't really seen each other outside of class, but when we do, he'd better say something. He didn't even show up!!! And he left me with a big problem!!! He'd better apologize!!!

Thursday, September 18   *Alberto's Journal*

Last night at dinner I decided to prank my dad. It was my job to pour lemonade for everybody, and when no one was looking I added some salt to Dad's glass. He made such a funny face when he tasted it that Esteban laughed and laughed! Whenever he stopped laughing, my dad took a sip and made the face again and Esteban would crack up again. We all laughed until our stomachs hurt and tears came out of our eyes. When we finally calmed down, I got Dad a new glass of lemonade. He took a drink and made the face even though there was nothing wrong with that glass and got us all going again!

I waited all week for Alberto to say he's sorry
for what he did to me. I felt like it was up to him
to make the first step since he's the person who
did the wrong thing. We don't see each other that
much, especially since I've been eating lunch in
the newspaper office so I can get some work done.
But he could have looked for me between classes
or called me or something!!! But he didn't!!! So I
had to take matters into my own hands yesterday
at lunch.

I finally had time to eat lunch in the cafeteria
so I sat next to Denver. I tried to talk to him
about how Alberto let me down, but he didn't
pay one bit of attention. He was busy playing with
that dumb game he got on his birthday. Which
he isn't supposed to have at school!!! It was like I
was invisible!!! I was already mad about the way
Alberto treated me and I didn't appreciate how
Denver was acting. I got fed up and said, "Excuse
me!!! How about a little respect???"

He looked up for just a second and back
down again and the game made this weird sound
and he yelled, "You made me mess up!!!" Then
he started playing again!!! That stupid game is so
mindless. He should do something educational
like I'm doing. I heard that one member of our
Brain Team moved away so I've decided to sign up
to take his place.

Anyway, Denver started playing again so I thought I'd just take my stuff and move someplace else if he was going to be like that. But then Alberto sat down with us which could have been his big chance to finally say he was sorry for leaving me waiting around the other day, but he didn't even mention it so I brought it up myself. Then he said he was sorry, but it didn't sound like he really meant it. I was so mad it felt like steam was coming out of my ears, but I just stuck some food in my mouth and kept quiet. You can't *make* somebody feel sorry for their actions.

Then Chantal came along and sat down and started getting on my case for missing youth group—like it was my fault!!! I patiently tried to explain the situation, but it didn't do any good. She kept griping at me, and Alberto agreed with everything she said. They just don't understand what it's like to have a busy schedule. They could at least be nice to me. I mean . . . we *are* friends!!! Well . . . we used to be such great friends, but now they are all making me mad!!!

Friday, September 19   *Alberto's Journal*

I hate it when my friends and I aren't getting along. Yesterday at lunch, Suki started complaining that I let her down by not showing up for Tuesday's interview. But she was the one who was late! I told her I waited for half an hour and then I had to go meet my friends, but she was still mad. I even said I was sorry and she was STILL mad! I didn't know what else to say to her.

Then Chantal sat down and she started complaining about Suki missing youth group again. But Suki said it was because of me! She said I ruined everything and she had to do something to take the place of my interview so that's why she missed youth group. Then I tried to defend myself and I said it was her own fault because she was late. Chantal agreed with me and then the girls started arguing about whether Suki is getting too busy. I agreed with Chantal and soon I was arguing, too. The only person who didn't get involved was Denver because he was playing his game. He never even looked up. I don't think he noticed we were sitting next to him.

At least things are good with football. Coach Pulaski keeps playing me and encouraging me, too. He's a tough coach and he expects us to work hard, but we all respect him and like him. That's why we're going to TP his house! When Osmond said we should do that, I didn't think it was a good idea. But he said the football team TPs the coach's house every year so it's like a tradition. "The coach expects us to do it sometime," he told us. So we all said okay. We're going to do it tonight!

After what happened yesterday, I'm not eating lunch with Suki anymore! She actually ARGUED with me like I'M the one with a problem when SHE is the one who's changed. I don't even know who she is anymore. And I'm not going to TALK to her ever again! I don't need a FRIEND like that. I need a REAL friend! Like somebody who CARES about people besides just HERSELF. And that person is NOT Suki! OBVIOUSLY!

I finally made it to the seventh level of Zplutz! I was really close at lunch yesterday, but Suki started talking to me and made me mess up which dropped me all the way back to the bottom. But last night I solved the last maze on the last door and it opened and I came through into a maze with glass walls! Now I have to do all the stuff I did in the other mazes, but sometimes I don't even know something is there until I run into it. If I bump into a wall, then I get dropped down. I don't know how many times that's happened to me already? It's going to be hard to make it through this level, but I have all weekend to work on it. If Mom lets me! She thinks I need to do other stuff like play outside and get some fresh air. Like we don't have air in our house! She just doesn't understand that you don't succeed at a game like Zplutz without putting in plenty of time.

Saturday, September 20   *Chantal's Journal*

Okay, I said I was NEVER talking to Suki again, but after I calmed down I felt like I couldn't just let our friendship die. We have been through a lot of stuff together. Like when my little sister Amanda was sick with her heart problems, Suki was really there for me. She has been a GREAT friend so I realized I had to try to work things out. Even though she is really the one messing up our friendship, I felt bad for how I talked to her the other day. I wasn't being a very good friend myself, was I?

So I called Suki and said, "Hi." And even though it is SO HARD for me to apologize for anything, I said, "I'm sorry, okay?"

She said, "I'm sorry, too."

Then I told her, "We need to talk."

And she said, "I know."

After that, we had a good, long talk. I told her about all the problems I'm having with babysitting and with my parents. She was so understanding about everything. She said she knew I would work things out which made me feel so much better.

Then Suki talked about how Alberto and Denver don't seem very interested in our group lately. I had to agree. Alberto is always doing stuff with his friends from football even when he's not practicing or playing a game. And Denver never stops playing that STUPID game! Suki said she tried to talk to Denver the other day, and he got mad that she interrupted his game. How RUDE is that? It's like the guys are hardly even our friends anymore. We decided we can't let things keep on like this. We're going to try to talk to Alberto and Denver about doing something together like we used to do.

Saturday, September 20 — *Alberto's Journal*

I talked to my parents about TPing the coach's house and they checked with the other parents and found out it really is OK the team does it every year. So I got to go with the rest of the team last night and it was really fun! Yazid's mom and Joey's dad picked us all up and took us to Coach Pulaski's house and helped us out. It seemed weird to have chaperones on a prank, but the parents always do that, I guess. Anyway, we sneaked around the coach's yard and quietly draped TP on his mailbox and his car and the bushes along his driveway. It looked like snow! Then we TPed the bushes up against his house. We tried to be quiet, but we couldn't help laughing sometimes. After that we started doing the railings on his porch. Suddenly, the light came on and the coach burst out of his front door, yelling, "What's going on out here?" For a second, I thought he was really mad, but then he laughed and said, "You guys better come in and have some hot chocolate."

So we went inside the kids and the parents too and Mrs. Pulaski made hot chocolate and the coach gave us cookies and we had sort of a party. It's so cool how the football team has all these traditions. They always TP the coach's house and he always gives them a treat and it all helps the team become a really tight group. I just have to thank God that I'm part of it all. It's a great experience!

Another tradition the team has is coming back the next day and cleaning up the TP. So I have to go do that now!

Week Six

BRAIN TEAM RULES!

St. Paul's amazing Brain Team easily defeated North Middle School's brainiacs in Saturday's competition. Tonight they battle with Central East! The epic fight takes place here at 6 tonight. Be sure to come and cheer them on!

Tuesday, September 23   *Suki's Journal*

Chantal and I are both worried about our group. We're just not as close as we used to be, and we want to do something about it. So when we all sat down to lunch at the same table yesterday, I decided it was time to take action!!! First, I told Denver to turn off his game because we had to talk about something and we had to talk about it right now. He didn't like that, but he did it. Then he sat there looking bored, which is how he looks a lot these days. I said that we are all busy and we're not doing that much together anymore and aren't we friends anymore? And then I said if we don't watch out our group is going to fall apart!!! Alberto and Chantal said I was right, and Denver changed his expression and agreed. Then he said, "But what can we do about it?"

I had already been thinking about that, and I said, "Let's have a game night at my house!!!" They all thought that was a good idea, and we tried to schedule a time we could do it. It wasn't easy, but we finally figured out we could have game night on Saturday, October 4. After we got it worked out, I had to hurry to the library to look around and choose our next book club book. I hated to take off like that, but I felt pretty good knowing things are going to be okay with me and my friends.

Tuesday, September 23   *Denver's Journal*

Suki is unbelievable! She wants us all to come to a game night at her house, which is a good idea, but she expects everybody else to arrange everything around her. I thought we'd never figure out a time to get together! Whatever night anybody named, Suki said she had something else to do. And she acted like whatever she had to do was more important than what anybody else had to do. She even tried to get Alberto to skip a football game so we could get together when she wanted. But did she offer to change any of her activities? Of course not! She really made me mad, but I took a deep breath and kept my temper under control. Our group just isn't as strong as it used to be, and Suki is right that we need

to get together. So I guess it's worth it
to go along with her?

Hey, since it's game night, I'm going to
bring along the best game of all! Zplutz!
Who knows what level I'll be on by then? And
Mom keeps making me put the game away
and do something else, so I could use some
playing time away from her eagle eyes.

Tuesday, September 23   *Alberto's Journal*

Suki is getting way, way, way too busy! We
all tried to set up a time we could get together,
and it was really hard to work around her
schedule. She didn't want to give up anything,
but she thought the rest of us should! Finally,
we found a time that would work, but I bet Suki
will be late even though it's going to be at her
own house.

Tuesday, September 23   *Chantal's Journal*

Oooh! Suki is so BUSY! Oooh! Suki is so
IMPORTANT! Oooh! Suki is getting on my
NERVES again! The rest of us have activities, too,
but she acts like the only thing that matters is
what SHE'S doing. But at least she's trying to
keep our group going. And the game night at her
house does sound fun.

I could really use some fun! Babysitting is
NOT fun at all. It's always a struggle to make

Harrison do what he's supposed to do when he's supposed to do it. I'm on his case all the time. Okay, not ALL the time but a LOT of the time. And even though I am the person in charge, Harrison doesn't seem to respect me. He does respect his parents because if I threaten to tell them something he straightens up for a few minutes. And he keeps asking me not to tell them about his behavior. So I haven't told on him and he hasn't said anything about me either, I guess. I keep praying for God to make that kid change, but so far it's not working.

I've also been asking God to make my parents change. They have so many rules for me that it's RIDICULOUS! And if I don't keep them EXACTLY, they just have to say something. Like it really matters if the bathroom is cleaned at the exact same time each week! And why shouldn't I watch a little TV before doing the dishes? And I know how to dress myself, okay? I know the styles, and they don't. When I try to talk to them about stuff, they won't listen. I can't wait until I'm grown up and out of the house!

BRAIN TEAM MOVES ON!

Central East's Brain Team didn't know what hit them Tuesday when St. Paul's own geniuses defeated them 53 to 2! The next challenge for our brave brains is defeating Middleton Middle School on their home turf this Saturday at 5. Come and support your fellow students!

Thursday, September 25   *Denver's Journal*

I used to think Mr. Santiago was a cool teacher. Social studies isn't my favorite subject, but he tried to make it interesting. And he was really nice in class and out of class, too. But now he's changed, and I don't like him anymore.

Yesterday he was talking to us about the ancient Greeks which is so boring. Like anybody cares about people who lived millions of years ago and dressed so funny! I slipped ?plutz? out, muted the sound, and started playing. I was really careful to keep the game behind my desk so Mr. Santiago wouldn't see it, but I guess he noticed that I never looked up. I couldn't or I might mess up the game! Suddenly, he was standing right beside me saying, "What are you doing, Denver?" I tried to hide the game under the desk, but he said, "Hand it over!" Like it was a cheat sheet and I was actually doing something wrong. Then he walked up to the front of the room and locked the game in his cabinet. Then he gave this little speech reminding everybody that handheld games aren't allowed in school because we're there to get an education, etc., etc., etc. Then he told me I could come by after school and get the game back but never to bring it to school again.

I think he made a big deal about nothing. It's just a game! And the class was boring anyway! I was so close to the next level. I bet I could have made it by the end of the day if he hadn't stolen the game from me.

Thursday, September 25   *Suki's Journal*

I got finished with my homework pretty early last night and I was going to research French restaurants online but Justin and Lee came barging in, begging me to play a game. Like I had time to for that!!! They got all mad when I said no and ran off and tattled and Grandma came to my room and asked if my homework was finished. When I said it was, she said, "Good! Then the whole family can play a game together. Come on!" Then she walked out before I could say anything.

When I got to the kitchen, everybody was at the table setting up a game. I said, "You guys go ahead without me. I have some other stuff to do."

Grandpa said, "I thought your homework was finished."

And I said, "It is, but I have other things to do."

"More important than spending time with your family???" asked Grandma.

Justin and Lee said, "Yeah!!!"

I said I didn't say that. I just needed to do some stuff for French Club and my other activities.

Grandpa said, "If you're too busy for your family, then you have too many activities."

I was afraid he was going to make me quit something so I said, "I'm not that busy. I can do that stuff another time. But I'm having that game night with my friends soon. That's why I don't want to play tonight."

Grandma and Grandpa both frowned at me.

"But that's okay," I said. "I'll play." Then I pulled up to the table.

Justin and Lee cheered and started arguing over who got what game token. Like it really matters who has the blue token or the yellow token or whatever!!! It took forever to get through the whole game because the boys are so slow rolling the dice and counting out their spaces. Then they wanted to play again and my grandparents said okay. I was going to get so much stuff done last night so I could get other things accomplished today, but now all my plans are messed up!!!

Thursday, September 25   *Alberto's Journal*

I can't believe what happened in PE yesterday! Denver, Osmond, Ray, Yazid, and I were playing on the same basketball goal, and some girls were playing on the next goal. When the teacher was at the other end of the gym, Osmond got this look on his face like he does when he's going to play one of his pranks. Then he faced the girls and yelled, "Hey, Amber! Yazid likes you!"

Yazid turned bright red! I mean bright red! Then he said, "No, I don't!"

Then Osmond said, "So you hate Amber now?"

Yazid said, "No!"

Then Osmond said, "So you do like her."

It was so funny and a lot of people were laughing, but all of a sudden Denver came up and shoved Osmond and said, "Shut up!"

Then Osmond shoved him back and said, "Why don't you make me?"

It looked like they were going to fight so I pushed between them and said, "Calm down, you guys!"

Denver stepped back, but then he looked at me and said, "Why are you hanging around with this idiot?" Then he walked off towards the locker room, and he didn't turn back even when the teacher asked him where he was going.

Osmond said Denver has no sense of humor, which is kind of true, but I wonder if he's having trouble at home again. Lately he seems tired and cranky and he was like that back when his mom had a drinking problem. I hope that's not happening again. I'm going to pray for Denver and his mom.

Sometimes I feel so lucky to have the parents I have.

Thursday, September 25   *Chantal's Journal*

I got this idea that I thought might help with Harrison. I made a poster of the rules I expect him to follow. I figure I can keep the poster in my pack and hang it on the refrigerator whenever I'm babysitting. Then if he does something wrong, I'll point to the rule and give him a timeout. I showed him the poster yesterday and started reading every rule to him and explaining each one. Before I even finished, he was breaking Rule #18—"No pretend yawning." When I pointed it out, he said he wasn't pretending and I was boring! So I made him sit on a chair facing the corner while I read the rest of the rules. I could tell he was still yawning, but I just ignored him. When I let him come back to the table, he behaved pretty well so I think my plan is going to work!

Harrison's Rules

1. Do what you are told.
2. The first time!
3. Eat your snack without complaining.
4. Don't complain about anything else either.
5. Say please and thank you.
6. Do a good job on your work.
7. Write neatly.
8. Do your work quickly.
9. But not so quickly that it isn't right.
10. Read your book correctly.
11. Read your book at normal speed.
12. Read your book loudly but not too loudly.
13. Do not smart off.
14. Do not argue.
15. Do not whine.
16. Respect the babysitter.
17. Do not insult the babysitter.
18. No pretend yawning!
19. No crawling under the table!
    Or other furniture.
20. Do not tip your chair back.
21. Sit up straight and listen.
22. No animal noises!
23. Do not roll your eyes.
24. Do not sigh.
25. Look at me when I'm talking to you!
26. **Just behave!**

Friday, September 26   *Chantal's Journal*

I don't think my plan is going to work. Yesterday, Harrison slouched down in his chair even though there is a rule about sitting up straight. (Sometimes that kid reminds me of Denver!) I got out the poster and pointed out that rule, but Harrison acted like he never even saw the poster before! I had to go over the whole thing again, and when I got finished he said, "Huh?" So I read it all again, but after each rule I made him repeat what I'd said. Then he wouldn't remember and I'd have to repeat it again. I could tell he was doing it on purpose. I guess he thought I'd just give up, but I didn't. I kept at it until he finally said the rules correctly. It was EXHAUSTING! I can't go through that every time! I just can't!

Friday, September 26   *Alberto's Journal*

I was going to try to talk to Denver today and explain to him that Osmond was just joking around yesterday. But every time I saw him, he looked like he was in one of his really bad moods. I'll just let him cool off a while before I try to talk to him. And maybe I shouldn't say anything about what happened in PE anyway. It just might make him mad again. There are a lot of great things about Denver, but his temper isn't one of them!

I really am getting pretty busy! Not TOO busy, like Chantal thinks, but PRETTY busy! I need to make a calendar or schedule or something so I don't forget to do something. Actually, it's kind of cool that I need to do something like that. It just shows that I'm accomplishing a lot in my life!!!

Week Seven

Monday, September 29

Before school—turn in video for morning broadcast, meet with Mademoiselle O'Reilly about
ideas for FC field trip

Lunch—finish article about lunch ladies

3:00—cover Art Club meeting

Tonight—homework, start studying for sci test,
research ss report, finish book club book and
write discussion questions

Tuesday, September 30

Before school—Brain Team practice, go to library
and find next book club book

Lunch—tape next video (interview a teacher?)

3:00—book club—discuss, intro new book

4:00—edit video, write article about Art Club

6:30—Brain Team vs. St. X

7:30—Youth group (if time!)

Tonight—homework, study for sci test, research ss
report

Wednesday, October 1

Before school—turn in video for morning broadcast, all newspaper articles, Brain Team practice

Lunch—last chance to study! Sci test after lunch!

3:00—library—finish up research for ss report

Tonight—homework, start writing ss report

Thursday, October 2

Before school—start book club book!

Lunch—free!!!   help Mrs. Pyle w newspaper

3:00—phone calls—restaurant for FC? Ad sponsors for newspaper?

Tonight—homework, finish writing ss report

Friday, October 3

Before school—newspaper planning meeting

Lunch—free!!!

3:00—catch up!!! Homework, report, read book,
etc., etc.

Saturday, October 4

9:00—nursing home

11:00—clean house, get ready for game night

2:00—finish book club book

4:30—Mass

6:30—party!!!

BRAIN TEAM NEVER GIVES UP!

Our big brains lost to Middleton Middle on Saturday, but they fought all the way! Middleton won by only two points! With its excellent record, St. Paul's Brain Team still has a good chance of making it to this quarter's citywide tournament. With a win there, they can move on to county, regional, and even state! It all depends on a victory over St. Xavier tomorrow. Come and see the crucial match here at 6:30!

Tuesday, September 30   *Denver's Journal*

I made it to the eighth level late last night—no thanks to Mom! She's always getting on my case about playing my game too much. She says I should develop other interests. Like anything could be as interesting as Zplutz! So I try to do other stuff when she's around and play when she's not paying attention. That isn't leaving me much game time so I have to sneak and play under the covers when she thinks I'm sleeping. Hey, who can sleep when you're in danger of falling seven levels at any moment.

This morning Alberto asked me if I wanted to go to youth group tonight. Like everything is okay between us. I said, "Why don't you ask that clown Osmond to go with you?" Then he said, "Come on, Denver. It will be fun." I told him maybe, but I don't know if I want to be friends with somebody who is friends with Osmond.

Tuesday, September 30   *Suki's Journal*

I am so nervous about our Brain Team competition tonight!!! This is a big one!!! Please, Lord, help us win!!! Please!!! Please!!! Please!!!

Tuesday, September 30   *Alberto's Journal*

I'm trying really hard to be friends with Denver, but he isn't making it easy. He's in a terrible mood all the time anymore. I'm worried about him. But I'm not going to ask him if his mom is drinking again. (I hope not!) You can't push Denver too much or he'll just shut down. Or explode! All I can do is be a good friend so he'll feel okay talking to me when he's ready.

We finally lost a football game. Of course, I'm disappointed, but my parents are still proud of me. And we could still make the championships. And of course it didn't change who we are as a team. Nothing can change that!

Things are still not going well with our group. Suki has hardly said TWO WORDS to anybody lately. I'd really like to talk to her, but she is just too BUSY! She's going to miss youth group again because of Brain Team. She might as well just QUIT youth group. It's not like she ever comes to meetings anymore. There's a lot of tension between Denver and Alberto. And Denver is crabby with everybody. I feel crabby, too. Thank goodness we are going to have a fun night together on Saturday! SOMETHING has to happen soon to save us!

My parents were happy to see that I got an A on the essay I did for extra credit in social studies. They thought it was really good the way I went and asked Mr. Santiago how I could bring up my grade. Dad said that was very mature!

Student Conduct Report

Date: *September 30*
Sent to office: *1:47*
Student: *Denver Jackson*
Teacher: *Mr. Santiago*
Class: *Social Studies*

This is the second time I've caught Denver playing a hand-held game in class. Last time he received a warning not to do it again, and I allowed him to have his game back at the end of the school day. When I confronted him this time, he was disrespectful and disruptive, claiming my class is "boring" and "a waste of time."

Action Taken: *detention, confiscation of game, parental contact*

Signed: *Mr. Webster, principal*

DATE: TUESDAY, SEPTEMBER 30, 7:22 PM
FROM: ALBERTO
TO: DENVER
R U COMING 2 YUTH GRUP?

DATE: TUESDAY, SEPTEMBER 30 7, 7:27 PM
FROM: DENVER
TO: ALBERTO
GROUNDED BCZ OF CONDUCT RPT SKOOL IS SO P911 GGN!

BRAIN TEAM MAKES TOURNAMENT!

With last night's victory over St. Xavier, our Brain Team has secured a spot in this quarter's citywide tournament! The competition takes place at 7 Saturday night in the high school auditorium. We're proud of you, brainiacs! Good luck!

DATE: WEDNESDAY, OCTOBER 1, 7:15 PM
FROM: SUKI
TO: ALBERTO, CHANTAL, DENVER
SORRY! BRAIN TOURN SAT. HAV 2 CHANGE GAM NITE. HOW ABT FRI 10/10?

DATE: WEDNESDAY, OCTOBER 1, 7:19 PM
FROM: CHANTAL
TO: ALBERTO, DENVER, SUKI
OK

DATE: WEDNESDAY, OCTOBER 1, 7:21 PM
FROM: ALBERTO
TO: CHANTAL, DENVER, SUKI
OK BY ME 2

DATE: WEDNESDAY, OCTOBER 1, 7:27 PM
FROM: DENVER
TO: ALBERTO, CHANTAL, SUKI
WHTEVER

I guess Suki is too busy to even talk to her friends in person anymore! Now she just texts us. It's ridiculous! Like she couldn't stop rushing around for one minute to speak to us? She wasn't even at the lunch table yesterday. At least I don't think she was. I didn't look around that much because I was busy battling my way to the next level of Zplutz.

I'm not supposed to have it at school— or at all actually. Since I got in trouble for playing in class, Mom took the game away for a while. Which I could kind of understand. But then she grounded me until further notice. How stupid is that? It's not like I did something really bad! I wasn't even bothering anybody! And then I got in trouble AGAIN for texting Alberto when I was supposed to be working on my homework. I tried to tell Mom that I promised Alberto I'd come to youth group and he had to be wondering why I wasn't there and it would be rude to just leave him hanging, but she yelled at me and took away my phone, too. She is being so unfair! So I didn't feel bad about sneaking the game out of her dresser and bringing it to school with me. If I don't keep playing, I'm going to lose my touch!

Yesterday was HORRIBLE! It seemed like Harrison was trying to break every one of my rules on purpose! It's not like you can just accidentally read in a duck voice! I pointed to Rule #22 and read, "No animal noises!" Then he oinked and said, "Okay." I lost my temper and yelled, "Oh, knock it off, you little pig!" He scrunched up his face and started crying—I mean he was really bawling! I told him I was sorry, but he wouldn't stop crying. I felt TERRIBLE! What kind of babysitter calls a little kid names like that? Then his parents got home and he ran to them and told them what I said. I started crying, too, which was SO EMBARRASSING! When I could talk, I told them I was sorry for losing my patience, but he wasn't obeying the rules. They saw the poster and they stood there and read it to themselves and shook their heads. They didn't look very happy. Harrison's mom said that maybe I wasn't ready to babysit and his dad said they didn't want me to babysit anymore until they talked to my parents. They will call them soon!

I knew if I said anything when I got home, I would just start crying again so I didn't tell my parents what happened yet. I felt like I needed to think about how to handle things. After Suki texted us about changing game night, I really wanted to talk to her about everything so I called her. She didn't answer even though she just sent out the texts! So she had to be IGNORING my call! When I got up this morning I had a text from her, saying sorry she was busy last night. Like that was a big surprise.

At least Alberto still knows what it means to be a friend. We talked before school this morning, and he really listened. It's no wonder the guys on the football team like him. He is really a nice person! And he agrees with me that Suki is way too busy. We talked about Denver, too, and how RUDE he is. He is even rude to the teachers. He slouches and yawns and acts bored just like he does when we try to talk to him. Alberto is scared that he's having trouble at home, like maybe his mother is drinking again, but I have another idea. I think he's playing that stupid game too much! Alberto said that he hopes I'm right. So do I!

Friday, October 3   *Denver's Journal*

I almost made it to the ninth level last night, but Mom came into my room and caught me playing. She was really mad that I took the game out of her dresser, and she took it again and locked it away in her file cabinet like it's something dangerous. She said I might NEVER get it back because she didn't think it was good for me. But she's the one who gave it to me! We argued for a long time until she said she had to go to sleep or she wouldn't be any good at work the next day. I went to my room, but I could hardly sleep at all because I WAS SO MAD!!!!!

Friday, October 3   *Alberto's Journal*

Denver looks really tired today. I tried to talk to him, but he just walked on by. His attitude is terrible lately—to the teachers and to his friends. Chantal thinks his game is affecting him, and I wonder if she could be right. Denver used to get in trouble in school, but he changed that and started doing fine. Then he got that game and he started playing in class. In class! And when his mom took the game away, his attitude got even worse. If that game means that much to him, then he really does have a problem. I wish I knew how to help him. I can pray for him, but what else can I do?

Friday, October 3   *Chantal's Journal*

I told my parents I didn't have to babysit yesterday, but I didn't explain why. I was going to tell them the truth, but then I CHICKENED out. Then later in the evening, Harrison's dad called and asked my parents to meet with them tonight to talk about how the babysitting is going so far. Mom talked to him and she thought it was a great idea. "It's good to stop now and then and evaluate," she told me and Dad. I agreed with her then made an excuse to go to my room. Obviously, Harrison's dad didn't say anything bad about me—YET! It's going to be AWFUL when Mom and Dad find out what I did. I feel SICK about the whole thing!

Friday, October 3 *Suki's Journal*

My brothers got me in trouble this morning!!! They wanted me to read them a story, but it was almost time for the bus and I was finishing up some homework. So I told them to go away and they went and told on me and my grandparents came and gave me a lecture about how I don't have time for my brothers or my friends anymore. I reminded them about the game night I'm having with my friends to prove them wrong, but they acted like that didn't mean anything at all and they kept talking and talking!!! Their lecture went on for so long that I missed the bus so Grandpa had to drive me to school but I was late for the special French Club meeting I called to discuss having another fund-raiser because I found out French restaurants are expensive and then I didn't have time after that meeting to make the special Brain Team practice session which is so important because we have the tournament tomorrow!!! Tomorrow!!! And I was already missing the newspaper planning meeting! Nobody appreciates how busy I am. If they did, they wouldn't waste so much of my time on unimportant stuff!!!

What is happening to our group? I thought Denver, Suki, Chantal, and I would be friends forever, but it's like we're falling apart! Yesterday we all sat at the same table for lunch, but we could have been on different planets. Everybody just sat there and ate without saying one word. They all looked really tired and depressed—completely different from my friends on the football team. Those guys are always joking around and laughing, and that's part of what makes our friendship work. So I thought it would be a good idea to do something to make everybody laugh. At first I was going to try Osmond's mashed potato trick on somebody, but I decided they all looked too crabby for something like that. Then I got the idea to play baseball with one of my carrot sticks and a pea. That would be so hilarious they'd have to cheer up! Well . . . that's what I thought anyway.

So I held the carrot like a teeny bat, tossed up the pea, swung, and missed. "Strike 1!" I yelled. It was really funny, but nobody laughed. So I tried again—and missed again. "Strike 2!" I yelled. Still nothing. They all just stared at me. I wasn't going to give up! I took one more swing, connected with the pea, and sent it sailing towards Denver. It hit him in the nose and fell into his mashed potatoes.

"That's it!" he shouted, jumping up so fast he knocked his chair over. "I'm sick of you and your stupid pranks!" Then he grabbed his tray and stomped off!

I turned to Chantal and said, "Uh-oh. I think I really messed up."

Her eyes filled up with tears and she said, "Me, too." Then she took her tray and left the table, too!

I looked at Suki, but before I could say anything, she said, "I don't have time for this." Then she left!

I felt terrible that I did something that upset everybody. But it's not just my fault, I know. Something is wrong with us. Really wrong. It makes me sad to think our group might be breaking up.

Saturday, October 4   *Suki's Journal*
- -

Please, Lord, help me do a good job at the tournament!!! Please!!! Please!!! Please!!!

Saturday, October 4   *Chantal's Journal*
- -

Harrison's parents talked to my parents and then my parents talked to me when I got home yesterday. At first, it was REALLY BAD. They started off with this huge lecture about how babysitting is a big responsibility. Then they said that calling Harrison a name showed I wasn't ready to babysit. Then I got upset and cried and Amanda started crying because I was crying and Mom looked like she was going to cry, too.

Finally, we all settled down and got Amanda playing with some toys and then my parents and I REALLY talked about things. I told Mom and Dad the truth about how badly things had been going, and they asked me a lot of questions about how I handled Harrison. Then they told me that being in charge of somebody never really works if you try to boss them around too much and control them.

"You can MAKE people do what you want," said Mom. "But they'll never really respect you."

"And then they try to fight back however they can," said Dad.

I had to admit that DID sound like what happened with me and Harrison. I thought I was doing what I had to do to get his respect. I mean . . . my parents boss me around! But I figured maybe I went a little overboard.

Then Mom and Dad told me some stuff I COULD have done. Like noticing whenever Harrison did something good. And setting up some kind of reward system. And talking to him firmly but RESPECTFULLY. They had lot of good ideas like that.

"I wish I could try some of that stuff," I said.

Mom and Dad looked at each other. Then Mom said, "I know you can do better."

And Dad said, "Maybe we can talk to Harrison's parents and see if they'll give you another chance."

I thanked them and hugged them and felt really happy for a while. But then I started thinking. What if I still have problems?

October 4, 11:17 am

Alberto: whats up Denver?

Alberto: hey, D!

Alberto: U busy?

Saturday, October 4   *Suki's Journal*
- -

Well, we lost the Brain Team tournament but only by three points!!! Grandma and Grandpa said we did a good job and they were proud of me for answering so many questions. I'm going to do a lot of extra studying so I can do an even better job next quarter and maybe we'll win the whole shebang!!! (That's not French. That's something Grandpa says.)

Week Eight

Monday, October 6

Before school—turn in video for morning broadcast, review for today's Eng test!

Lunch—interview band teacher for newspaper

3:00—French C—finalize plans for bake sale

4:00—auditions for play

Tonight—homework, make sci vocab cards, research English paper

Tuesday, October 7

Before school—sign up for Art Club, write up interview

Lunch—help Mrs. Pyle w newspaper

3:00—tape next video (football practice)

tonight—get supplies for fall decorations at nursing home, edit video, catch up on studying!!

7:30—Youth group (if time!)

Wednesday, October 8

Before school—turn in video for morning broadcast, read book club book

Lunch—write Eng paper?

3:00—follow-up phone calls—newspaper ad sponsors

Tonight: — homework, study sci voc (test tomorrow!), work on nursing home decorations, bake!

Thursday, October 9

Before school—bake sale

Lunch—bake sale, study sci voc!

3:00—count $, turn in to Mlle O'R, cover Sci Club

Tonight — homework, write up Sci Club, clean house for game night

Friday, October 10

Before school—meeting w Mr. Webster—TV station plans

Lunch—help set up Art Club show

3:00—make food for game night, set up, finish nursing home decorations

7:00 Game night! Party!

Saturday, October 11

9:00—nursing home—take decorations!

11:00—catch up!! Homework, study, finish book club book, do painting for Art Club, plan next video, any articles?

3:30—Confession (if time)

4:30 Mass

Tonight—catch up!!

I IM'ed Denver Saturday to see if he wanted to go to the Brain Team tournament with me, but he didn't answer. I figured he was still mad at me about the prank I played on him, but when I saw him this morning he said, "Sorry I couldn't IM you back. Mom only allowed me on the computer for schoolwork." So I said it was okay and then I apologized for the prank even though I thought he could have had a better sense of humor about it. He said it was okay, but I think he still seems kind of mad. He'll be ungrounded on Friday, in time for Suki's game night—if he doesn't get in trouble again! He couldn't act more bored in his classes, and the teachers are really fed up with him. I wouldn't be surprised if he got sent to the office again.

I talked to Chantal, too, and said I was sorry if I upset her on Friday. She said she was just stressed out, not to worry about it. I asked her why she is stressed, but she changed the subject to our math homework. Friends should be able to talk to each other about their problems!

I wish Mom would give me my game back.
I'M SO BORED BORED BORED BORED BORED
BORED BORED BORED BORED BORED BORED
BORED BORED BORED

I'm WORRIED about babysitting again. The first thing I'm going to do when I see Harrison is apologize. That isn't easy for me to do, but I know I have to do it. I hope he can forgive me and we can start over again. I've been thinking a lot about how I can be positive with Harrison like Mom and Dad said and say nice things and be patient. I'm going to make a chart for him with the things he needs to do. Every time he does something, we can mark it off and I can say something good about him. That way I'll be saying positive stuff instead of yelling at him. I hope it works!

Monday, October 6, 5:42
To: <Mrs. Lewis>
From: <Suki>

>Dear Mrs. Lewis,

>I am so sorry about what happened
>today. I got behind on my school
>work and I was trying to catch up. I
>know we were supposed to be writing
>in our journals, and I shouldn't have
>pretended that I was. I won't do it
>again!!! I'm very, very, very sorry!!!
>Suki

Monday, October 6, 7:48
To: <Suki>
From: <Mrs. Lewis>

>Dear Suki:

>I appreciate your apology, and I know I can
>count on you! Mrs. Lewis

Monday, October 6, 7:52
To: <Mrs. Lewis>
From: <Suki>

>Thanks so much!!! See you tomorrow!!!
>Suki

Tuesday, October 7 ★★School News★★

BRAIN TEAM STILL OUR CHAMPIONS!

After a great season, the Brain Team lost in the early rounds of Saturday's tournament. Of course, they put forth a fantastic effort, which makes them winners to us! We can't wait to see what they do next quarter!

Tuesday, October 7 *Suki's Journal*

I don't think I did a very good job at the play tryouts yesterday!!! I never got around to picking up a script so I could practice ahead of time and I had to read lines that I never saw before and I messed up a lot. But I'm already pretty busy so I guess it will be okay if I don't get a part. I mean . . . I can't do EVERYTHING!!!

Tuesday, October 7 ★★School News★★

Come to Le Café de Paris!!!
Enjoy delicious treats at the French Club Bake Sale!!!
Thursday, October 9

Wednesday, October 8 *Chantal's Journal*

Harrison's chart is ready and I am, too. Well, as ready as I CAN be. I made the chart really cute with some animal stickers and I bought some stick-on stars that I can put in each section. I've planned out everything I'm going to say when I get there today. I have to make it sound like things are going to change and I'm going to do a better job and we're going to have more fun. I have to remember to BE POSITIVE!

I wish I felt POSITIVE about Suki. I don't think she's EVER going to make it to youth group EVER again.

☺ Harrison's Do a Good Job List ☺

Walk home
Eat snack
Do homework
Read book
Play!

Wednesday, October 8   *Alberto's Journal*

Things still aren't good with my old friends.
At youth group last night, Chantal kept complaining about Suki, who wasn't there, of course.
We never even see Suki anymore! Denver is still
dragging around with a terrible attitude. I am
praying for game night to bring us all back
together again.

At least things are good with my football
friends. Really good! We're still having lots of
laughs. Like yesterday in PE. Osmund brought
some peanut butter to the locker room. He gave
it to me and told me about this cool prank. He
distracted Ray while I dipped a pencil in the
peanut butter and very gently dabbed it onto
the back of his shorts. How funny is that? And
when we all ran out to the gym, people noticed
the peanut butter and they started pointing

and laughing so hard that some of them actually fell on the floor. Ray didn't know what was going on. It was hilarious! Finally he twisted around and looked at the back of his pants. His face turned instantly red and he ran out. It was really, really funny! Later Ray came back with some new shorts on and his face still looked red, but that could have been because he was running. I mean it probably was because he was running. He was running pretty fast.

| Wednesday, October 8 | *Denver's Journal* |

Osmond is a jerk! Osmond is a jerk! Osmond is a jerk! Osmond is a jerk! Osmond is a jerk! Osmond is a jerk! Osmond is a jerk! Osmond is a jerk! Osmond is a jerk!

| Wednesday, October 8 | *Suki's Journal* |

Mrs. Lewis is such a nice teacher. Sometimes I think I would like to be a teacher like her! Of course, I don't want to give up my dreams of being a filmmaker and a reporter and a chef, but maybe I'll get some kind of teaching in there somewhere. Hey, I know!!! After I'm a famous director, I can teach a course for people who have the same dream. Or maybe I could have my own TV show where I teach people how to cook delicious French food!!!

I didn't get a part in the play, but that doesn't mean I can't be a famous actress some day. I'll just have to work on that later when I have some time.

Thursday, October 9   ***Chantal's Journal***

    Babysitting was better yesterday! Not PER-FECT! But a LOT BETTER! Harrison hugged me when I apologized and said, "That's okay." Wasn't that sweet? And he really liked the chart once he got the idea of it. Every time he did one of the things on the chart correctly, I made a big deal about it and told him how good he was and put a star on the chart. He still argued with me some, but I kept my patience and encouraged him and . . . IT WAS SO MUCH BETTER! When I got home I told Mom and Dad about how things went and they said I was getting the idea and they're proud of me for trying again. I'm actually looking forward to babysitting this afternoon!

Thursday, October 9, 3:57 pm
To: <Suki>
From: <Mrs. Lewis>

>Dear Suki:

>I know this is short notice, but one of the
>Poetry Club members can't make it to the
>slam tomorrow night. If it's okay with your
>grandparents, would you like to go along in
>his place? Please check with them and let
>me know. Mrs. Lewis

Thursday, October 9, 6:59 pm
To: <Mrs. Lewis>
From: <Suki>

>Dear Mrs. Lewis,

>That would be great!!! My grandparents
>say it's okay. Thanks for asking me!!! Suki

DATE: FRIDAY, OCTOBER 10, 7:27 AM
FROM: SUKI
TO: ALBERTO, CHANTAL, DENVER
SORRY BUT SUMTHNG CAME UP! HAV 2 CANCEL GAM
NITE. ILL CHCK SKED & GET BACK 2 U W NEW TYM

DATE: FRIDAY, OCTOBER 10, 7:33 AM
FROM: CHANTAL
TO: ALBERTO, DENVER
CAN U BLIEV IT? Y TXT US?

DATE: FRIDAY, OCTOBER 10, 7:37 AM
FROM: DENVER
TO: ALBERTO, CHANTAL
WE NVR C HER @ SKOOL!

DATE: FRIDAY, OCTOBER 10, 7:42 AM
FROM: ALBERTO
TO: CHANTAL, DENVER
I NU THS WUD HAPN. SHES 2 BZ!

DATE: FRIDAY, OCTOBER 10, 7:45 AM
FROM: DENVER
TO: ALBERTO, CHANTAL
LETS JUST DO IT RSELVS B4 I GET GRADED AGN!

DATE: FRIDAY, OCTOBER 10, 7:50 AM
FROM: ALBERTO
TO: CHANTAL, DENVER
OK MY HOUS 2MORO NITE

DATE: FRIDAY, OCTOBER 10, 7:53 AM
FROM: CHANTAL
TO: ALBERTO, DENVER
OK. SHUD WE TELL S?

DATE: FRIDAY, OCTOBER 10, 7:55 AM
FROM: DENVER
TO: ALBERTO, CHANTAL
Y BOTHR?

DATE: FRIDAY, OCTOBER 10, 7:57 AM
FROM: ALBERTO
TO: CHANTAL, DENVER
SHELL B 2 BZ 2 COME ANYWAY

DATE: FRIDAY, OCTOBER 10, 8:01 AM
FROM: CHANTAL
TO: ALBERTO, DENVER
OK C U THEN! & @ SKOOL 2!

Week Nine

The poetry slam was so much fun!!! I even got up and read a poem. I had to write it at the last minute, but it wasn't half bad. It goes like this:

Tick tock tick tock
I can hear the clock!
Tock tick tock tick
That clock is much too quick!
Hurry hurry
I have to scurry
But don't you worry
I can beat the clock!
Tick tock tick tock!!!

Afterwards, people came up to me and said they really liked it. Oh, and it was cool to ride in the school van with the other kids and Mrs. Lewis. She is really nice!!! Since I didn't get into the play, I think I'll join Poetry Club instead. I like writing poems even though I haven't written that many of them.

Yeah, the slam was great, BUT!!! I really should have been working on my schoolwork and my other activities. I had to spend the rest of the weekend catching up. But now I'm in pretty good shape. I made my schedule for this week, and it looks like I might even be able to go to youth group tomorrow. That should make Chantal happy. And my grandparents, too. I didn't go to confession on Saturday because I just had too much to do! Grandma and Grandpa got all upset when they found out about that! They told me that I'm too busy and I'm not spending enough time on important stuff and my faith is very, very, very important. Like I don't know that!!! So, anyway, they'll like it that I'm doing something at church!!!

Monday, October 13

Before school—turn in video for morning broadcast, review for today's ss test!

Lunch—interview Mr. Webster for newspaper

3:00—Art Club—turn in painting

Tonight—homework, prepare book club questions, start health poster

Tuesday, October 14

Before school—go to library and find next book club book, write up interview

Lunch—help Mrs. Pyle w newspaper

3:00—book club—discuss, intro new book

tonight—edit video, catch up on studying!! Finish health poster

7:30—Youth group (if time!)

Wednesday, October 15

Before school—turn in video for morning

broadcast, start book club book

Lunch—write ss essay

3:00—French C—finalize plans for field strip

Tonight—homework, make name tags for
FC field trip, write poem

Thursday, October 16

Before school—everything ready for field trip???

Lunch—FC field trip!!!

3:00—write up interviews and TURN IN!!!

Tonight—homework, write up field trip for
newspaper, catch up chores

Friday, October 17

Before school—review for today's sci quiz!

Lunch—library—research ss bio

3:00—practice reading poem, homework,
start ss bio

7:00 Poetry Slam!!!

Saturday, October 18

9:00—nursing home

11:00—catch up!! Homework, study, finish book
club book, plan next video, any articles?

2:00—cover football game

4:30—Mass

Tonight—catch up!!

Game night was okay, but it didn't fix things with our group. I don't know why I ever thought that it would. How could it fix our group when we weren't all there? It didn't seem right having the games without Suki. It was like we were keeping a secret from her. What kind of friends do something like that? I hope she doesn't find out what we did or her feelings are going to be hurt.

Denver wasn't there either—not really! He came to my house, but he brought his game which he just got back from his mom. That would have been okay if we all could have played the game, but Denver wouldn't let Chantal and me touch it. We kept asking him if we could play, too, and he kept saying we could after he got to the next level. I tried to trick him into giving it up, but it didn't work. By the time he finally got to the next level, his mom was there to pick him up. He walked out the door still playing the game!

At least Chantal and I played some board games with each other and talked like friends. But it just wasn't that much fun without the others.

Suki and Denver don't even know what it means to be a friend. They don't care about our group, and they are just plain old RUDE! Suki is rude because she canceled out on us at the last minute and then expected us to rearrange our lives around her—AGAIN! Like she's the queen of the world! And Denver is RUDE because he spent the whole game night playing by himself on that stupid Zplutz game! He barely even talked to me and Alberto, and when he did, he was mad because we were distracting him from reaching the next level like that was CRUCIAL. I told him IT'S JUST A GAME, but he was too busy playing to listen to me.

The only one who is still a REAL friend is Alberto. He let us have the game night at his house after Suki canceled and he made a lot of good food for us and he was really nice. He and I played some games and talked about stuff. I told him about my problems and he was very understanding. He was impressed with my plans to improve things with Harrison, and he's sure they will work out. I think he's right. Harrison really IS doing better! I just wish my parents would quit asking me stuff about every little thing that happened while I was babysitting. I don't need all that PRESSURE! Last night I got so tired of it that I said, "Do you have to keep interrogating me?" They told me to watch my attitude, but why don't they watch theirs?

I don't know why I even went to that stupid game night? The snacks were good, but Alberto and Chantal kept interrupting me while I was playing Zplutz. I mean . . . over and over and over! I told them I was trying to make it to the ninth level, but that didn't stop them. I said they could play later. But they kept distracting me! Alberto even went out of the room and came back with the phone and said my mom wanted to talk to me. I told him I wasn't falling for it because the phone never even rang. Him and his stupid pranks! He never learns!

The rest of the weekend was lousy, too. Mom only let me play my game for a few hours. I need a lot of practice to make up for all the time I missed, but there's no point in telling her that. She'll probably get mad and take it away again.

I am so upset!!! My friends aren't really friends at all!!! They are a bunch of two-faced, sneaky liars!!! I feel so stupid that I ever trusted them!!!

I found out the truth yesterday. I worked really hard over the weekend so I would be caught up so I could finally go to youth group again. I even asked Chantal if I could come to her house after book club since my grandparents had something at the boys' school and wouldn't be able to take me to youth group. Now that I think about it, she wasn't that friendly when she said okay. I should have realized something wasn't right!!!

When I got to her house, I went to her room and we started on our homework. After a while, Chantal left to get us a snack. I noticed her journal on her desk and I wondered if she had written anything about me, like I wondered if she still thought I was too busy. Of course, I know you shouldn't read somebody's journal, but I just thought I'd take a teensy little peek. And it's a good thing I did!!! I found out that my so-called friends had a game night at Alberto's house WITHOUT ME!!! They didn't even invite me!!! And then they kept it a secret!!! How can they treat me like that??? I was going to yell at Chantal when she came back, but just in time I realized that wasn't a good idea. She would wonder how I suddenly found out and she might figure out I looked in her journal. And even though it wasn't really such a bad thing to do considering what I found out, I didn't want to start an argument. Me looking in her journal wasn't really the important issue. So I told her I forgot something I had to do and went home. I'll talk to those traitors later!!!

I'm so glad this day is almost over, but before I go to bed I HAVE to write about it. Our group EXPLODED at lunch today! Alberto, Denver, and I were all at the same table, and Alberto and I started talking about how we should try to do something else together soon. And I said maybe something fun outside. (I was thinking that Denver couldn't play his game if we were hiking or something like that.) Then I asked Denver what he thought, but guess what? HE WAS PLAYING THAT GAME! He totally ignored me, and I yelled at him and said he wasn't supposed to have it at school. He said what did it matter since he wasn't in class.

"Aren't you in enough trouble already?" I asked him.

He started getting mad and asked what did I mean. So I started talking about how he acts bored with everything but his game and he has a terrible attitude. Then Alberto got in on it and said he agreed with me and he said Denver must be addicted to the game or he wouldn't be breaking the rules by bringing it back to school again.

Denver started yelling about how that was NOTHING compared to the stuff Alberto and his "gang" are doing. He said that they are just mean jerks.

Then Alberto got mad and started yelling about how Denver doesn't know what's funny and why does he have to be so cranky all the time LIKE

A LITTLE BABY! I thought he had a point so I said, "Yeah!"

We were all so busy arguing that we didn't see Suki roll up until she shouted, "I want to talk to you people!" Somehow she found out that we had game night without her and she was MAD! We told her that we just did it because we're sick of her ridiculous schedule and the way she treats us. She said that we were the ones who didn't know how to treat a friend and then she took off. Denver said, "No kidding!" Then he left, too.

I looked at Alberto and said, "How did Suki find out?"

He said, "Are you accusing me?"

I said, "No! But somebody told her."

"Well, it wasn't me!" he said. Then he left!

Why does this stuff keep happening to us? It was just TERRIBLE! We never used to argue like this. Well, okay, we had some disagreements, but it wasn't like this.

I was still upset about it when I got to my babysitting job. Wouldn't you know this would be the time that Harrison would start acting up again? It was almost like he knew I had other stuff on my mind. He tried to go through his math worksheet and just write down any old number without actually doing the problems. I started yelling at him like I used to, but then I realized what I was doing. I stopped to take a deep breath and then I told him firmly BUT CALMLY that he had to erase and start over. I even said, "I

know you can do it, Harrison. And I'll help you."
He folded his arms and sat there and pouted. It
was so CHILDISH I felt like screaming! There was
a time I probably WOULD HAVE screamed at him
and just made the situation worse. But this time
I said, "And when you're finished, we'll put a star
in that box and then we can play a game." And he
got to work!

I'm so tired, but before I go to bed, I'm going
to pray and ask God to save our group. I can't lose
my friends!

Thursday, October 16 *Suki's Journal*

I don't care if I ever talk to Chantal or Alberto or Denver ever again!!! They are not my friends
anymore and I'm not going to waste one more
minute on them!!! I have plenty of stuff to do
without them!!! I HATE THEM!!! And I'm going
to have fun on the French Club field trip today
eating fancy French food and I'm not even going
to think about them!!! C'est fini! (It's over!!!)

Thursday, October 16 *Alberto's Journal*

I have always been a good friend to Denver
even when he was acting terrible. And now he
says my friends and I are mean jerks. He's the
one who's a jerk! That's what Osmond said when
I told him what Denver said about us, and I hate
to say it but I have to agree. Osmond says we
don't have to take that and we should do some-

thing to get back at him. We talked awhile and we came up with a great plan. Well, really Osmond thought of it, but I'm going to help him. I'm going to stay over at Osmond's tomorrow night. After it's dark, we'll sneak up to Denver's house and paint "JERK!" on his garage door! It's not like graffiti or anything. We're just doing it to teach him a lesson. It's just a prank that he really deserves.

Thursday, October 16 *Chantal's Journal*

Everybody is still mad at everybody else this morning. I tried to talk to Suki, but she just ignored me! PLEASE, Lord, help us!

Thursday, October 16 *Denver's Journal*

That is so ridiculous that Chantal and Alberto think I'm addicted to Zplutz! I'm not playing it in class anymore and I'm getting all my work done. The game hasn't affected me at all except for the fact that I'm really getting good at it. I'm on the tenth level, and it is so cool! Now there's some kind of monster that grabs you, rips a hole in the floor, and throws you down to the first level. It's really hard to avoid him because he's invisible until he actually touches you. It scares you to death because he's a big ugly blob with a bunch of arms and one big eye bulging out! There must be some way to tell when he's around, but I haven't figured that out yet.

A Poem by Suki

I thought we were friends,
friends to the end.
But all of you lied
and tossed me aside.
You were cold-hearted,
and now we have parted.
We're no longer friends.
Yes, this is the end!!!

Friday, October 17   *Chantal's Journal*

None of my friends are talking to each other, and I'm not talking to them either because if they're not going to talk to me then why should I talk to them? But I have to say that I really miss them! Especially Suki. I'd like to talk to her about what happened with my parents last night.

Yesterday babysitting was the best ever so I was feeling pretty happy when I got home. But as soon as I walked in the house, my parents told me they wanted to talk to me. We sat down in the living room and they started getting on my case about my chores. I haven't been keeping up with them very well lately, but I've been just a teensy bit STRESSED, okay? And just when I got my babysitting problem solved, the trouble with my friends got worse. The LAST thing on my mind is getting my chores done. So I got mad and said, "Oh, I'm sorry! My life is falling apart, but I guess you don't care about that as long as the carpet gets vacuumed!" My parents said all this stuff about how they did care and what was wrong and could they help, but I folded my arms and said, "Never mind."

Dad frowned and said, "I think you're a little old to be pouting like that."

"I'm not pouting!" I cried. But then I realized he was right. I was being just as childish as Harrison! I dropped my arms and said, "I'm sorry." Then I told them about some of the stuff that was happening with my friends. We talked awhile and they helped me feel more hopeful that things will work out. Then they helped me catch up on my chores. Which they didn't have to do. They could have made me do them all by myself.

It really made me think. My parents are strict, but they care about me. And, really, they try to treat me the same way they told me to treat Harrison— with some respect. I guess I'll never like all the rules and being told what to do and all that, but I should have a better attitude around home. I'm going to work on that!

Friday, October 17   *Suki's Journal*

Okay, this is the weirdest night I've had in a long time! I don't have anything to do!!! I joined the Poetry Club and I was planning to go to a slam tonight. Grandpa was going to take me, but when we went out to the car, it wouldn't start. It was too late to call somebody else for a ride so I couldn't go. I went to my room, thinking I'd do some homework, but it's all caught up! I read over my report for social studies so I'll be ready to present it to the class next week, but that only took a few minutes. Our French Club field trip is over, I already did my next video, and I have everything turned in for the newspaper! I wasn't about to call Chantal or Denver or Alberto after the ridiculous way they treated me!!!

Then I thought, *Hey, the boys are always bugging me to do something with them!* So I went to their room and asked if they wanted to play a game. They said no!!! And I asked them why not because all they were doing was coloring.

Justin looked at me and said, "We're busy!!!"

Lee said, "Yeah!!!"

Then they went back to coloring.

I said, "Fine!!!" Then I went back to my room and tried to read a book, but I was too mad to concentrate. I tossed the book aside and started thinking. How could my brothers be too busy for me??? Didn't they care anything about my feelings??? Well, if they were too busy for me then I was too busy for them!!!

That's when I realized something. Usually I *am* too busy for them! How many times have they wanted me to do something with them??? And how many times have I turned them down because I had other stuff to do??? I felt bad when they didn't have time for me. I must have made them feel bad a hundred times. Maybe even a thousand!!! I feel terrible about that!!!

And now I'm wondering if my friends were right when they said I've been doing too much stuff. Have I made them feel bad, too???

And you know what? I love my activities, but it felt kind of nice to have nothing to do for once!!!

Saturday, October 18   *Denver's Journal*

I wish I could just live inside my game. At least it gets me away from all the problems in my life! Like Alberto and his gang. When I went out this morning to bring in the paper, there was graffiti on our garage! It said, "JERK!" I bet Alberto told Osmond what I said and the whole group came over and did that. And I'm sure Alberto was in on it. He has completely changed, and I'm never going to be his friend again!

If Zplutz was real and I really lived in that world, I wouldn't have to deal with my mom either! I told her about the graffiti and she came out and looked at it and freaked out. She asked me if I knew who did it, but I'm trying to talk to her as little as possible so I just shrugged which made her mad.

Then we went inside and had breakfast and she went off on me because I started playing my game. But she was reading the paper so what did it matter?

I really, really, really wish I could live in my game instead of going to school. It's so boring! And annoying! I had to give my oral report in social studies yesterday, and Suki and Chantal slouched in their seats and yawned and acted bored the whole time. Why can't everybody just leave me alone?

Saturday, October 18   *Suki's Journal*

Today my life was back to normal—busy, I mean!!! I volunteered at the nursing home this morning like usual, and in the afternoon I covered the football game for the newspaper. Our team lost, but Alberto made a touchdown so I decided to interview him. I thought he'd give me some good quotes, but he didn't seem happy about the touchdown at all. When I asked him what was wrong—as a friend, I mean, not a reporter—he said he was afraid his friendship with Denver was over for good!!!

I told him, "Well, what do you expect, Alberto??? You called him a baby. Why should he be friends with you when you disrespect him like that???"

That made Alberto mad and he said, "Oh, yeah??? Well, maybe that's why nobody is friends with you anymore!!! You're always too busy to show us any respect!!!"

Last night, I thought a lot about how I've been acting and I knew Alberto was right so I said, "I know. I've been doing that at home, too. I'm sorry, okay?"

After that we talked about how we could fix things with our friends. We decided we have to apologize first thing Monday morning!!!

Week Ten

Sunday, October 19 *Alberto's Journal*

I think I ruined my friendship with Denver. I should have never insulted him like I did the other day. I got mad and I said stuff without thinking and I shouldn't have done that. Suki thinks an apology will fix everything, but she doesn't know about what Osmond and I did the other night. I thought it would be a good prank to paint something on Denver's garage, but it wasn't! I should have known that when Osmond and I had to sneak out of his house to do it. It wasn't like when we TPed the coach's house and all the parents knew what we were doing. But Osmond said it wasn't a big deal he did it all the time and we were just playing a prank. I thought, Yeah, it's just a prank. And I tiptoed out the back door with Osmond and followed him to Denver's house.

It all seemed fun and exciting and funny at first. But when we finished painting and I saw that great big J-E-R-K on Denver's garage, I knew we had done something really wrong. Painting on a building isn't just a prank—it's vandalism! And it wasn't funny at all to call Denver a name like that. He's going to suspect Osmond for sure—and probably me, too. And I'm afraid he'll never forgive me. I really messed up! Suki is right that I should apologize, but I don't really think it's going to work.

Suki came up to me at my locker this morning and said she needed to talk to everybody. I opened my mouth to say I didn't want to talk to her, but Denver walked by and she grabbed him and said the same thing. He looked like he was going to argue with her, but Alberto ran up then. I was surrounded so I shut my locker and just stood there until she said whatever she had to say. She opened her mouth, but Denver whipped out his game and started playing it! Alberto asked Denver to stop and listen. I don't think Denver was going to do it, but Mr. Webster came walking down the hall so he had to put it away. That's when Suki started talking.

I was surprised when she actually apologized for how she's been acting! She said she realizes she has been doing too much and she's cutting back on her activities because her friends and family are important to her. Then Alberto apologized for having the secret game night, and I did, too, and Denver said, "Yeah." Suki said it was okay.

But the apologies weren't over yet! Alberto apologized to Denver for playing a prank on him, and Suki and I apologized for how we acted during his report. Denver accepted our apologies, but I think he's still kind of mad—especially at Alberto. And he said we are wrong about him being obsessed with his game. Then he took it out and started playing again! We all gave him annoyed looks, but he didn't notice.

I don't think everybody's really over all the stuff that happened, but now that we've apologized to each other, I think we can heal our friendships. It's a start at least!

Monday, October 20 — *Suki's Journal*

It was really, really, really, really hard to apologize to my friends, but I did it. I got everybody together before school and told them I'm sorry about the way I've been treating them. And they forgave me and they started talking to each other again! I hope everything will be OK now!!!

Monday, October 20 — *Alberto's Journal*

This morning I told Denver I was sorry about painting the stuff on his garage, but I still feel terrible about it. And I think maybe he's still mad at me. I wish I could think of some way to make him forgive me!

Monday, October 20 — *Denver's Journal*

Everybody's sorry for everything. At least, that's what they all say. I guess I should forgive them, but I don't know if I can. I mean . . . the girls think I'm some kind of game addict or something and ALBERTO VANDALIZED ME! It's not easy to forgive stuff like that. Yeah, they're sorry, all right.

Now I'm in study hall and I feel better because I came up with an idea to help make things right. I told Denver about it at lunch. I said I would come over this evening before supper, apologize to his mom, and paint over the garage door. He said, "Whatever." Then he took out his game and played it the rest of the lunch period. But maybe he'll forgive me once I take care of things tonight. I think he will!

Mrs. Jackson was pretty mad when I said I painted the door, but she did accept my apology and let me fix it. I used some leftover paint from our shed. I didn't see Denver the whole time I was there. His mom said he was in his room doing his homework. Right! He was playing that game, I bet.

I did see Osmond. He walked by while I was out there working. Mrs. Jackson was on the porch then so he didn't stop and talk. But he called me later and asked what was going on. When he found out I didn't tell on him, he thanked me and started talking about what we could do to Denver next! I said our pranks were getting out of hand and it wasn't right and I wasn't going to do stuff like that anymore. He said that pranks are our team thing, and I won't really be a part of team if I don't do pranks.

I started to tell him that painting the garage wasn't just a prank, but he hung up on me.

I figured he was pretty mad, and I was right. When I opened my locker this morning, I found out that somebody had squirted shampoo into the slits and messed everything up inside. I bet it was Osmond!

DATE: TUESDAY, OCTOBER 21, 7:22 PM
FROM: CHANTAL
TO: SUKI
YG STARTNG!

DATE: TUESDAY, OCTOBER 21, 7:29 PM
FROM: CHANTAL
TO: SUKI
WHERE R U? U SED UD B HERE!

DATE: TUESDAY, OCTOBER 21, 7:32 PM
FROM: CHANTAL
TO: SUKI
I THGHT U WERE GOING 2 CHANGE!

Wednesday, October 22   *Chantal's Journal*
- -

I can't believe that Suki! She promised me she was coming to youth group last night, but she didn't show up and she didn't call or text or ANYTHING! She SAYS her friends are important, but I'm not sure she really MEANS it.

Chantal is mad at Suki because she missed youth group again. I told her she needs to give Suki a chance because it is hard to change. Chantal said she understood that. Like it's taking a while for her to change how she acts when she's babysitting. And around her parents, too. She said she'll try to be patient with Suki. They've had their ups and downs before, and I think they'll work everything out and things will be okay between them. Deep down, they are really good friends!

I wish Osmond and I could work things out and be friends again. There was a picture of a rat taped to my locker this morning, and the locker was full of shaving cream when I opened it. I tried to not care, but it made me feel bad. Now I am so sorry for the pranks I was involved with before. I made people feel the same way I feel now and I wish I hadn't done that! I'm glad I changed and quit doing that stuff. I wonder if Osmond could change.

I'd kind of like to tell my parents about the stuff Osmond is doing to me, but if I tell them that then I'll have to tell them what I did to Denver's garage. I thought Denver's mom would call them about it so I didn't say anything but she didn't call and now I don't want to tell and make my parents upset.

Denver is so busy with his game that I can't tell if he's mad or not! But I think he is.

Wednesday, October 22   *Denver's Journal*

I have defeated the blob! Man! That took forever! I finally figured out that even though the monster is invisible he leaves a trail of purple slime on the floor. On to Level 11!

Thursday, October 23   *Chantal's Journal*

Hey, I just realized that I didn't see Suki all day yesterday! And I haven't seen her today either. She must be sick. Maybe that's why she missed youth group and didn't answer my texts. I shouldn't have assumed she was letting me down. I hope she's better soon!

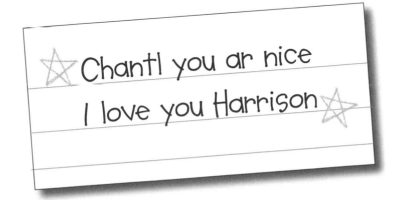

Chantl you ar nice

I love you Harrison

I think Osmond is turning the rest of the team against me. Nobody was very friendly at practice yesterday. And afterward, when I came out of the shower with just a towel on, my clothes were gone! Everybody laughed at me, and Osmond said, "Did you lose something?" Then Yazid nodded his head towards the trash can and I looked inside and there was my stuff. I quickly got dressed and got out of there before Osmond could prank me again!

Wow!!! I have had a terrible flu!!! I was too sick to even talk to Chantal when she called to check up on me. My brothers have been so nice, bringing me drinks and soup and stuff. I'm glad I decided to spend more time with them. They are good kids!!!

I feel a lot better today—and I don't just mean because the flu is gone. When I apologized to everybody the other day, I left out something important. I knew things would never be all right until I took care of that, and today I got my chance when Chantal brought me my make-up work. (It was so nice of her to do that!)

She explained some of the assignments to me and we talked awhile and then she stood up to go. I thought I'd better act right then before I lost my nerve. So I said, "Wait! I have to tell you something." She sat back down and I told her about how I peeked in her journal that time. I said I was really, really, really, really sorry!!! And could she ever forgive me??? She said she could! So I know our half of the group is really together again. If only we could get the boys back! Things still seem tense between them—at least whenever Denver isn't fooling around with his game.

Week Eleven

I really wanted to stay home from church this morning, but Mom said no and we got into a big fight about my so-called attitude problem. It was the same old stuff! I'm disrespectful to her and my teachers don't like how I'm acting and, of course, I play my game too much! We would have argued more, but we had to go because it was getting late. We just slid into the last pew as Mass started. It was almost the end of the service before I realized I wasn't paying any attention to anything. I was all zoned out, just sitting there planning out my strategy for the next level of Zplutz! I couldn't believe I was disrespecting God like that! That's when I realized everybody must be right about me and my game. I prayed and asked God's forgiveness and then I asked for his help. I need to make a change and it won't be easy!

When we got in the car afterward, I told Mom I was sorry about our argument. And I promised her I was going to quit playing my game so much. She hugged me and said she was proud of me. And then she asked me if it would help if she put the game away for a while again. I swallowed hard and said yes! This whole day has been terrible without it. I don't know what to do with myself and I feel totally bored. But I have to keep trying to get this thing under control.

Monday, October 27   *Alberto's Journal*

Last night somebody (I think I know who) left a bag of dog poop on our front step. I stepped on it this morning when I was going out to the bus stop. It was nasty! I had to quickly change shoes and run like crazy to the bus stop. All the way to school, I was feeling terrible and wishing I could talk to somebody about my problem with Osmond. When I got to school, I saw Denver and I went up to him and said, "I have a big problem."

He said, "So?" Then he walked off!

So he hasn't really forgiven me. I guess our friendship is over for good!

Monday, October 27   *Chantal's Journal*

Things are still not right with Alberto and Denver. Denver wouldn't even talk to Alberto this morning. This just can't go on or they'll never be friends again. I have an idea about how to get them together again, but I'm not sure if it will work. I'm going to talk to Suki about it. If she agrees with me, we can get the guys together and fix this thing today!

Alberto,
   meet in the courtyard
at lunch. It's important!
      Chantal

Denver,
   meet in the courtyard
at lunch. It's important!
      Chantal

Monday, October 27　　　　　*Suki's Journal*

Chantal had a great plan to work things out between the boys. She wrote a note to each one, saying to meet her, and we put the notes on their lockers. Once we had them together, we were going to tell them about how I betrayed Chantal's trust by reading her journal but she forgave me and now we're friends again so why can't they forgive each other? The only problem with the plan was that Alberto and Denver didn't show up! Our group is finished!!!

Tuesday, October 28	*Alberto's Journal*

Our group is back together! Yesterday when everybody was headed to the cafeteria for lunch, Denver saw Osmond fooling around with my locker. He ran and got Mr. Webster and they came back and caught Osmond gluing the edges of the door. That wasn't going to work, but it still made a big mess. Mr. Webster took Osmond to the office and sent Denver to get me.

I was on my way to meet Chantal in the courtyard, but Denver stopped me and told me what happened. I thanked him for helping me like that, and he said he was sorry about being crabby that morning. He's trying to give up Zplutz and he's having a hard time. (Which just proves we were all right that he had a problem!)

I went to see Mr. Webster in his office. Osmond and Coach Pulaski were in there, too. The coach said that he might kick Osmond off the team, and Osmond looked really upset so I said I didn't want that to happen and I could forgive him. Osmond looked really surprised —especially when the adults said okay. So he's going to clean up my locker and stay on the team. The coach said he's going to have a talk with the team about pranks. I'm really glad about that!

And I'm glad things are okay between me and Denver. I figure we can start doing stuff together again and that will help him get adjusted to life without Zplutz.

Now I just have to talk to my parents about the vandalism I did and everything will be OK again. Well maybe not OK exactly but at least I'll feel right. Even if I get a punishment from them. Which I will!

Tuesday, October 28   *Denver's Journal*

Sometimes I think Alberto is too nice. Osmond has played a bunch of tricks on him, but Alberto forgave him. But, hey, he's forgiven me a lot of times! I don't always appreciate it, but I know I'm lucky to have a friend like him.

I was supposed to meet Chantal in the courtyard at lunch yesterday, but I forgot. This morning I asked her what she wanted, and she said to never mind. Sometimes the girls drive me crazy!

Tuesday, October 28   *Chantal's Journal*

The guys are friends again! They were talking this morning just like they used to. I guess they met up on the way to the meeting. So my plan worked!

Tuesday, October 28   *Suki's Journal*

Chantal's plan didn't work, but Alberto and Denver are friends again anyway. I'll have to ask them sometime how they worked that out.

Now that we're all back together again, I'm going to have a game night at my house. FOR REAL!!! This time I won't let my friends down. I'm not going to do that ever again!!!

Youth group tonight!!! I'll be there for sure!!!

Suki

Mrs. Lewis
First Period English
St. Paul Catholic School

The Journal Project Wrap-up

We've reached the end of our journal project. Please reread your journal and write a paragraph below that describes what you learned from this experience.

Writing in this journal helped me see that my priorities were messed up. I was so busy with so many activities that I was actually neglecting my family and friends. I was even rude to people, and I don't want to be like that. I've cut out some activities so now I can respect what's really important in life!!!

Alberto

Mrs. Lewis
First Period English
St. Paul Catholic School

The Journal Project Wrap-up

We've reached the end of our journal project. Please reread your journal and write a paragraph below that describes what you learned from this experience.

I thought the journal project was just about English, but now I understand it was about more that that. When I look back, I can see where I really wasn't being honest with myself. I was disrespecting property and people, too, but I told myself it was all in fun. I just didn't want to admit it when I crossed over the line. Now I have a whole new attitude! And some new friends, too!

Denver

The Journal Project Wrap-up

We've reached the end of our journal project. Please reread your journal and write a paragraph below that describes what you learned from this experience.

I learned I don't like writing in journals, but it wasn't all bad. My punctuation is better I guess? When I read over my journal, I realized that I got more involved in my game than real life. That's not right. And that's not the way to treat other people. And I'm not going to do that anymore.

Chantal

Mrs. Lewis
First Period English
St. Paul Catholic School

The Journal Project Wrap-up

We've reached the end of our journal project. Please reread your journal and write a paragraph below that describes what you learned from this experience.

Writing in a journal has been GREAT! It's cool how a journal saves your life on paper! I forgot about some stuff that happened to me until I reread my journal. I can actually tell that I have gotten more mature since the beginning of the year. Now I understand that respect is a two-way street! And I really appreciate my friends since I came so close to losing them. I'm going to keep writing in my journal so I'll always have something to help me remember what happens to me and my friends. Not that I'll ever FORGET Suki, Denver, and Alberto! Thank God I have such GREAT FRIENDS!

Your Own Journal Project

The *Stepping Stones* kids wrote in journals as a school project, but you don't have to wait for an assignment. You can start a personal journal on your own! Journaling is good for improving your writing skills, expressing your feelings, and saving your memories. And it's fun, too!

Here are some tips for making journal writing a great experience:

1. You can buy blank books or diaries, but a regular notebook works just fine. Personalize your journal by decorating the cover with stickers, photos, or anything else you like.

2. Make writing in your journal something special. Set aside time for journaling and sit in a comfortable spot when you write. Use a cool pen, play music, or do whatever helps you enjoy the experience.

3. Journals are good for writing about what's happened to you, but don't stop there. Include your thoughts and feelings about the events in your life. That's what makes a journal really personal!

4. As Mrs. Lewis suggests, don't worry too much about grammar, punctuation, and spelling. Just do your best and keep writing! If you're concerned about something, check it out later.

5. You can keep your journal completely private or share parts of it with other people. It's up to you!

6. Journals aren't just about writing. You can draw pictures in them, paste in clippings from magazines, or create a comic strip about your life. Be creative!

7. If you don't know what to journal about, write your name or another word over and over (the way Denver

did), copy a poem, or write out the lyrics to a song you like. After a few minutes, you'll probably relax and think of a topic. Or if these suggestions don't work, try one of these ideas:

Writing Ideas for Your Journal

★ Tell about the funniest thing you ever saw.

★ If you could have one magical power, what would you choose? What would you do with your power?

★ What blessings do you have in your life?

★ Who is your hero? Why?

★ The best idea I ever had was . . .

★ What would you do if you were the President of the United States?

★ List ten things you don't like about your family.

★ List ten things you do like about your family.

★ What makes someone a good friend?

★ Write a prayer to your favorite saint.

★ I would never . . .

★ What famous person would you most like to meet? Describe your imaginary meeting.

★ It really bugs me when . . .

★ How would you describe yourself? How would you like other people to describe you?

★ Tell about your worst nightmare.

★ Write a letter to God about something that's worrying you.

About the Author

After over twenty years as a special education teacher, Diana R. Jenkins became a freelance writer. She has written more than four hundred stories, comic strips, and articles for children and teens as well as three books of children's plays, including *Spotlight on Saints! A Year of Funny Readers Theater for Today's Catholic Kids.* This is her first novel. Diana lives in Montgomery, Ohio, with her husband, a medical physicist.

Stepping Stones
The Comic Collection
Written by Diana R. Jenkins
Art by Chris Sabatino

Denver, Chantal, Suki, and Alberto are on a journey—and you can join them! With these fun and inspiring comics, you'll share the ups and downs, problems and joys, successes and failures of a great group of friends. The stepping stones of their lives are leading them on a path toward God.

Won't you follow along? After all, you're on that journey, too!

Paperback
128 pp.
71184
$9.95 U.S.

Anna Mei, Cartoon Girl

Written by
Carol A. Grund

No matter what her name sounds like, Anna Mei is *not* a cartoon character. But she *is* the new kid at school, and that just wasn't in the plan.

How's she ever going to fit in with the other sixth graders when she has a weird name, an adoptive family she doesn't remotely resemble, and an unknown birth mother somewhere back in China? She figures she'd better get busy transforming herself into someone who's less . . . unusual. After all, a pretend life is better than no life. But just when it looks as though Anna Mei 2.0 has everyone fooled, a school project comes along that makes her think about herself, her friends, her family—and that weird name of hers—in a whole new way.

Paperback
144 pp.
07885
$8.95 U.S.

Who are the Daughters of St. Paul?

We are Catholic sisters. Our mission is to be like  Saint Paul and tell everyone about Jesus! There are so many ways for people to communicate with each other. We want to use all of them so everyone will know how much God loves us. We do this by printing books (you're holding one!), making radio shows, singing, helping people at our bookstores, using the Internet, and in many other ways.

Visit our Web site at www.pauline.org

BOOKS & MEDIA

The Daughters of St. Paul operate book and media centers at the following addresses. Visit, call or write the one nearest you today, or find us on the World Wide Web, www.pauline.org

CALIFORNIA
3908 Sepulveda Blvd, Culver City, CA 90230	310-397-8676
2640 Broadway Street, Redwood City, CA 94063	650-369-4230
5945 Balboa Avenue, San Diego, CA 92111	858-565-9181

FLORIDA
145 S.W. 107th Avenue, Miami, FL 33174	305-559-6715

HAWAII
1143 Bishop Street, Honolulu, HI 96813	808-521-2731
Neighbor Islands call:	866-521-2731

ILLINOIS
172 North Michigan Avenue, Chicago, IL 60601	312-346-4228

LOUISIANA
4403 Veterans Memorial Blvd, Metairie, LA 70006	504-887-7631

MASSACHUSETTS
885 Providence Hwy, Dedham, MA 02026	781-326-5385

MISSOURI
9804 Watson Road, St. Louis, MO 63126	314-965-3512

NEW YORK
64 West 38th Street, New York, NY 10018	212-754-1110

PENNSYLVANIA
9171-A Roosevelt Blvd, Philadelphia, PA 19114	215-676-9494

SOUTH CAROLINA
243 King Street, Charleston, SC 29401	843-577-0175

VIRGINIA
1025 King Street, Alexandria, VA 22314	703-549-3806

CANADA
3022 Dufferin Street, Toronto, ON M6B 3T5	416-781-9131